At the Table

At the Table

A HEARTFELT CONVERSATION
ABOUT INFERTILITY

Amber Mitchell

PALMETTO
P U B L I S H I N G
Charleston, SC
www.PalmettoPublishing.com

Copyright © 2024 by Amber Mitchell

All rights reserved

No portion of this book may be reproduced, stored in a retrieval system, or transmitted in any form by any means—electronic, mechanical, photocopy, recording, or other—except for brief quotations in printed reviews, without prior permission of the author.

Paperback ISBN: 979-8-8229-3788-8

TO MIKE:

My best friend, husband, lover. I wrote this book to encourage those who are hurting. Thank you for being that person for me, for your continued patience and readiness to listen, and for gently pointing me back to God when I lose my footing. Thank you for the parts of you that balance the weak parts of me. I'll love you forever.

To my babies in heaven:
I think of you every day. Mama loves you.

There are three things that are never satisfied,
four that never say, "Enough"
the grave, the barren womb,
land, which is never satisfied with water,
and fire, which never says, "Enough!"
—Proverbs 30:15, 16 NIV

Consider what God has done:
Who can straighten what he had made crooked?
When times are good, be happy;
but when times are bad, consider;
God has made the one as well as the other.
Therefore, a man cannot discover anything about his future.
—Ecclesiastes 7:13, 14 NIV

Table of Contents

Prologue	ix
Meet the Mitchells	1
Journey	7
Rest	14
Anger	24
Seen	35
Share (The Eve Effect)	45
Boundaries	55
Where'd That Come From?	63
Marriage	75
Friendships	86
Advice	97
Untitled Intentionally	107
Works Cited	110

Prologue

In the middle of what felt like the never-ending season of unanswered questions and uncertain direction surrounding our infertility, my dad asked me how I could be patient while waiting on God for His timing and answers. I was surprised! I had never considered that I came across as patient! A few days went by, and as I sat with his question, it brought to mind an argument years before. A couple of friends from high school were dog sitting for me while I went on a family vacation. When I got home, there was a disagreement which led to my friend telling me, "Everything comes easily to you."

I often wonder if people have developed a perception that I have a composed, tidy life and the key to peace and patience. This impression couldn't be further from the truth. The reality is, each day is an opportunity to make a conscious commitment with the Lord to practice the habit of patience and look for peace in challenging places. Some days I'm more successful than others. As I write this, my husband, Mike, and I are considering starting a business, looking at purchasing our first home, and praying about how growing our family may or may not look. Dad's question was vital for me to answer because it helped me verbalize why I will continue to return over and over to my faithful God.

Here's how I responded:

I have seen a pattern in my life where growth with God has consistently been during difficult times. I've come to realize the goals we are striving for—opening a business, buying a home, and potentially involving ourselves in foster care or adoption—are mere chapters in a bigger story. That isn't to say they're less critical or unworthy goals; however, when I take a giant step back, I see God is teaching me more about myself through the lens of infertility. He's creating our story to have a foundation where we can trust God for a lifetime.

When Mike and I learned we couldn't have children, I was devastated and angry. I was confused why God would place us here, struggling with questioning His reasons and mourning His answers and, at times, what felt like His silence. Our pain, questions, and worries have nothing to do with proving ourselves to God. I often feel disappointed in myself when I am struggling emotionally, like that is somehow evidence I don't trust God. But these times are how relationships grow through honesty and allowing God to show us what He has in store, even if it is entirely different than what we imagined. Healing started the moment I wearily came to understand only the Lord could mend my broken heart, tenderly restoring it with dreams that aligned to His purpose for me. His choices and our circumstances are not a punishment for Mike and me (or you).

The truth is, my greatest fear has nothing to do with whether He'll answer my prayer for children, but that I could potentially allow my circumstances to change my attitude toward Him and ultimately embitter my heart. I had been too caught up in trying to steer what direction we were going, desperately grasping for control; I couldn't see the direction we were headed: aimless and sinking.

I've developed a deep relationship with God through this experience. He is a loving Father who is heavy hearted for His daughter. He's patiently nurtured endurance, strengthened my resilience, and placed a peace in me that exceeds understanding. He has led me to sacred spaces to mourn, to learn, to heal.

I tell you this because I am betting you're in a similar place of heartache and waiting. I wrote *At the Table: A Heartfelt Conversation about Infertility* because I hope to widen your outlook on what is possible with God and what He can reveal during the most challenging times in life. This book is a piece of my heart that I am giving you, filled with lessons, stories, and unfiltered honesty because I realize it doesn't serve me to strive to make this sound pretty. In fact, in doing so, it would make me downright disingenuous. Mike reminds me that people don't need "perfection"; they need candid honesty and vulnerability.

I set this project down for weeks because impostor syndrome had set in, and Satan convinced me that to be qualified to write and publish this work, I had to no longer be affected, have hard days, or second-guess all my options.

But this book isn't a directive about how to overcome infertility's emotional, physical, and mental adversity. I have my bad days, but thankfully they have come less and less. My phone's screen is shattered because I threw it on a hard day. I was frustrated about a medical bill that had come due, nine months later, to the tune of over a thousand dollars, requiring us to move money out of savings, leaving me feeling defeated. Less money in our savings meant a step backward in reaching our goals. Rage built in my chest as I squeezed my phone, throwing it right at the wooden leg on my couch. My tantrum created hundreds of tiny fractures on my phone's screen, adding insult to injury. I have not taken the phone in for repair yet. I want those spidery lines to remind me that anger produces impulsive actions, making what I am trying to look at incredibly unclear—life lessons from a phone.

I am not perfect, nor do I walk around as if my life is all together. However, I have peace that I am in the right place, even though I am hurting, and God is with me. So are you.

Here's to working on the anger.
Here's to working on the sadness.
Here's to giving a purpose to the pain.
Here's to doing this together.
Here's to living while we wait.

I want to share a personal rendition of Psalms 88 I reimagined a few days after our diagnosis. It was a Tuesday morning, and I was watching the wind blow in the month of September, bringing with it the promise of fall, my favorite season. Instead of appreciating the change of seasons going on outside my window, my mind was busy repeatedly going over the moment we were told we couldn't have kids. It was the first day I truly cried for hours, sitting in my chair, clutching my Bible in this private moment. When I was able to read, I went to Psalms, and I felt a connection to David's desperation, mixed with faith in the hope of God. I needed to tell God how lost and guilty I felt despite my professed faith, and with the help of David's psalm, I was able to. I was completely unaware this would be the beginning of a love story, but God was.

Psalm 88

O Lord, God of my salvation,
I have cried out day and night before You.
Let my prayer come before You,
Incline Your ear to my cries.
For my soul is full of troubles,
my soul melts from heaviness.
I am like a girl with no strength
who You remember no more.
I am looking for You, my God;
I cling desperately to You.
Please give me Your hand,
for I am losing my grip.
You have laid me in the lowest pit,
and my eyes are tired from crying.
My mind goes in circles trying to discern Your plan.
I want You to justify Your decision, knowing that it's unfair of me to ask.
I hate myself for not being strong enough to trust You readily.
I am a weak, desperate believer, undeserving of the blessings You've given me.
"One more."

My life is complete by Jesus, not the "one mores."
My heart is full of grief,
my head full of the unknown.
Lord, I am calling daily upon You;
I am stretching out my hands to You.
This is the hardest thing I've ever done.
This is my offer: here are my dreams, God,
my sweet desires, the most precious pieces of my heart.
At this moment I give these all to You.
I can't promise I won't try and take them back,
but I do believe they're better with You.
Perhaps You'll remold them or save them for another time.
I am desperately seeking Your faithfulness, Your lovingkindness in this darkness.
Shall Your wonders be known in the dark?
And your righteousness is seen by the forgotten?
Oh, turn to me and have mercy on me!
Give Your strength to Your servant!
Show me a sign for good.

Meet the Mitchells

Mike and I met when we were thirteen while at a party of a mutual friend. We bounced into each other in a bounce house; if you ask Mike, he'll tell you this was intentional on his behalf. His blue-gray eyes and self-assured smile gave my stomach plumes of butterflies! We dated through our freshman year, breaking up in the spring because Mike was apprehensive about Christianity and my genuine relationship with Jesus. Three years later, Mike came into the bakery I worked at, inviting me to see him play his guitar at an open mic night. Friends and I went, and Mike boldly performed a song he wrote for me entitled "Girl of My Dreams." As an invitation to our senior prom, he placed chocolate Kisses in the shape of lips on my bedroom floor and a card reading, "Now that I kissed the ground you walk on, will you go to prom with me?"

We built a wonderful, meaningful friendship as we dated. We grew together, maturing into adulthood, intentionally expressing how we felt and open to listening to one another without judgment. Mike never missed a moment, big or small, to support me when I needed him. He ran to my grandma's bedside the night she died, sitting with me for hours after, holding my hand. Mike hunted down a book I mistakenly returned to the library to find a special memorial bookmark I had left in it by mistake. He held me while I cried uncontrollably the first time I hit a raccoon while I was driving. He was and always has been my everyday hero.

On May 22, 2011, Mike proposed, accidentally kneeling straight down on broken glass as he asked me to marry him. Freely, he cried as I walked down the aisle, making me feel like the most beautiful bride in the world. To this day, that is one of the best moments of my life. Eight years went by quickly: birthdays, military, one bachelor's degree, overnight hotel stays, laundry, cleaning house, holidays, vet visits, vacation…life is fun, unpredictable, and challenging, but with Mike, even the mundane is special.

In March of 2014, I miscarried at six weeks; I didn't even know I was pregnant. I had a fleeting suspicion but had been busy working two jobs and planning my older sister's baby shower. Mike was working late, and I was frosting cookies for the shower when severe cramping and heavy bleeding started. I immediately took a pregnancy test, which registered a positive result, while I tried to comprehend what was happening. I couldn't fully wrap my head around receiving a positive pregnancy test and what the bleeding meant. My brain jumped from shock to fear, paralyzing thought and movement.

Mike got home a few hours later. I came around the corner, unable to speak, hugging him as I sobbed. I cried uncontrollably. I couldn't even keep myself standing, and he held me on our living room floor while he coaxed out of me what was wrong. At the exact same moment, I had to tell the love of my life and my best friend he would've been a dad, but I was miscarrying. With the tiny amount of medical knowledge I have, I was aware there was no intervention this early in pregnancy. Burying my feelings and without telling my family what I was going through, I left for Tennessee the next day for the baby shower. After my trip, I came home and scheduled an appointment with my gynecologist to ensure my body had passed all the tissue, avoiding any risk of infection. There I was met with a callous directive to lose weight before attempting to get pregnant again.

A year later we decided we wanted to start trying to have a baby. Since the miscarriage, my desire for a family grew, making me anxious and antsy. A couple of months quickly passed, and I started thinking, "Maybe this month" and planning, "If we get pregnant now, we can announce then, and our due date will be here, and it'll all fall into place so perfectly!" We chose to go to the fertility specialist after eight months without success. I was confident I was overreacting, and we'd find if we stopped obsessively thinking about getting pregnant, it would happen. You know, the typical advice you get from people.

Our insurance coverage at the time allowed testing, but after diagnosis, they would not cover any procedure or medications. Through research, I found there were three main treatment options:

1. Intrauterine insemination (IUI), which involves placing sperm directly into the uterus, costing upward of a thousand dollars* plus medication.

2. In vitro fertilization (IVF), which involves egg and sperm collection, with the fertilization process occurring "naturally" by mixing the eggs and sperm in a petri dish; then, after determining an embryo was created, reinserting it into the body. The average cost is about twelve thousand dollars a cycle,* not including the cost of medication, storage of unused embryos, or other potential medical care.

3. Intracytoplasmic sperm injection (ICSI), which Mike and I would learn would be the advised route in our case. ICSI is similar to conventional IVF, with an added step of having an embryologist use a fine glass needle to inject a single sperm directly into each egg. Then after determining viable embryos, the rest of the original IVF procedure would be followed. ICSI increases the cost of IVF by another two grand,* making the total come to fifteen thousand[1] for the procedure alone.

Due to our insurance coverage, we understood financially we would be responsible if treatment became neces-

---

[1] Costs have increased.

sary. Through extensive testing, we found our issue was sperm quality, and our case was referred out of our original infertility office to a specialist in reproductive urology in Chicago. The urologist discovered Mike's testosterone was drastically below average and prescribed us Clomid, which is known to increase testosterone in males. The doctor advised us to make another appointment in two months to retest Mike's hormone levels.

We sat on the train headed into Chicago eight weeks later, holding hands with a mixture of apprehension and hope around us. Mike's levels had increased dramatically! The doctor optimistically commented he wouldn't be surprised to see us pregnant by our next visit to our local clinic in a few more weeks! We went out to dinner to celebrate, calling family about the positive news. I remember being shaky because we had the potential to be pregnant by the end of the year, and although that's what we wanted, the thought was surprisingly overwhelming.

At our retest appointment, four days before our fifth wedding anniversary, we were told the medication had been successful for his increase in testosterone, but the treatment had not been effective for his sperm quality. I asked the doctor how it was possible to have gotten pregnant two years ago, and he replied, "Can you run faster now than you did two years ago?" What did running have to do with this? I remember feeling hollow, as if I were a husk of a body moving in slow motion, detached from the moment. As the doctor continued with our options and advice to "go about our life," I fought the urge to get up from my chair and walk out without stopping. I'd heard enough; my heart and mind were working overtime processing, trying to find something optimistic to say and coming up empty. Staying seated took all my strength and energy.

As I write this out, the feeling of hopelessness and heartbreak of those moments is fiercely fresh. Who could fix this? I had life planned out! How could it not go my way? Why us? How could I start to reassure my husband while trying to process the numbness that had just descended on me?

Mike Tyson once said, "Everyone has a plan until they are punched in the mouth," and doesn't that just say it all! I fell in love with this quote because it reminded me how I conveniently had life planned out: when we would have kids, what our home would look like, how we would spend our years in retirement. I wish I were kidding you. I have been driven and goal-oriented since my teens. Naivete is the biggest casualty of youth, and the unexpected is the most significant devastation to a meticulous planner. What I am trying to get at here is that I had been double punched!

The real question now was, "Am I going to allow infertility and the disruption to my plans stop what God was going to do through this?"

Journey

In the beginning, our diagnosis was crippling, and the only way I knew how to function was to grow numb, keep my head down, and move through the paces. Even now, years later, I still get stunned when I think about the reality of our circumstances. The first year after our diagnosis, I wrestled with depression. Being able to have a baby seems like a natural right. Multiple times in the Bible, God calls people to "be fruitful and multiply." Why is there infertility at all? I feel like any time I open Facebook or the news, someone somewhere has killed their children, and I want to scream, "Give them to me!"

Conversations about teens getting pregnant, spouses not engaging with their children, and moms complaining about the hardships of being moms make me feel like they don't fully appreciate their children. I know that isn't fair or true; however, I want to tell them to shut their eyes for a moment, think about their children's heads resting on them as they sleep, the laughter that fills their home, and the sweetness of these innocent faces that are half theirs and half their husband's. Picture those moments of simple joy gone.

Intellectually I understand this thought process is the grief talking. Those women have every right and all the knowledge to come back with how they struggle with lack of sleep, juggling schedules, and the ever-revolving door of plastic toys. When going through infertility, it's difficult not to romanticize being a mom. Motherhood is beautiful, messy, fulfilling, hard…it's so many things. However, my arms are empty, my house is quiet, and I would sincerely love to be able to have the "she has your mouth, my eyes" conversation with my husband. I still have to avoid anything that may remotely look like it needs nurturing because I will bring it home. In other words, *do not show me a puppy*! Motherhood feels like a club I am surrounded by and unfairly excluded from all at once.

Romans 8:28 says, "And we know that in all things God works for the good of those who love him, who have been called according to his purpose."

How are you going to work good from this God? Look at me: I fake happy Amber more days than not; I arbitrarily place judgment on women who justifiably struggle with the problems of motherhood. I physically and emotionally ache for children. What good can come from this pain? Right now, I can't even see past it.

As I read or listen to women speakers, I hear the word *journey* a lot. When I hear it used, I usually picture a grand, daring adventure. Dictionary.com defines it as "traveling from one place to another, usually taking a rather long time." Using this definition as a guide, we can see that a *journey* is neither a positive nor negative word, but it describes the place between.

I know I am on a journey I didn't plan for that feels relentlessly unforgiving. I have often had this conversation with Mike about how I feel like our life right now feels unendingly stagnant. We have lived in the same place since I moved out at twenty-one. I have gone to the same job every day since I was nineteen, and my weeks have become tedious. The exception being my spiritual life. Despite all the monotony, my spiritual life is anything but unchanging. I am drawing closer to God than I ever have before. I am learning to praise and worship in the bad times too. I feel like I roll from one Holy Spirit lesson to another like a wave in the sea. The other things—the home and the job—have become tools Satan uses on me so I become more involved in comparing my life with others, rather than the truth revealed by my Father. Nothing about growth is easy. I'm learning the importance of rest, how to be honest about this pain, where to set boundaries, how to protect my marriage, what friendships look like, the difference between good and bad advice, what worship and praise look like on hard days, and finally where my hope resides.

However, these days can feel as heavy and barren as a desolate wasteland. Imagine a day suffocatingly hot, oppressively preventing my ability to take in a complete cleansing breath. A land visibly parched, veined with red crevices, with dust encrusting my face without the help of any wind. The land stretches far and wide with no relief in sight, making me instantly exhausted at the immense effort it's going to take to traverse it. Loneliness envelopes me as I start moving, and soon, thoughts produce emotions: fear, sadness, anger, jealousy, and resentment. Aimlessly I wander, hoping my resolution not to be overcome by my circumstances isn't futile. I stumble accidentally upon a banquet table I almost miss because I've convinced myself it's a mirage, a cruel trick.

I have no idea how it got here, considering I haven't been looking for it and should've seen it with how exposed the terrain is. It's beautiful. It is a rustic table with gorgeous, soft, white flowers decorating its length, delicious and savory food covering the rest of the tabletop. Inviting pristine white china and crystal glasses, filled with the crispest, coolest water I have ever tasted sit sweating, waiting to be drunk. I eat to my heart's content, recognizing the sweetness at this moment. I relish in this sacred space as I snuggle into an oversize plush chair placed at the head of the table. I relax for the first time in miles, a sigh escaping my lips, a genuine smile slipping onto my face. Benefiting from this break, I can appreciate my surroundings—how the red earth makes the cloudless blue sky more radiant and the heat makes the cool water feel perfectly satisfying.

Without warning, the ground begins to tremble, and at first, I'm lulled by its vibration, but the movement builds quickly, creating anxiety and the knowledge I no longer feel secure. Millions of angry fire ants march in tight colony formation across the table, coating my much-needed bounty. I'm forced to move onward, back across the ruthless ground. This is how infertility, with all the decisions, emotions, and interactions, feels. Long stretches of unimaginable travel with slow progression and lavish secret encounters with Jesus that leave me feeling peaceful until I start moving again.

I am learning to give my perfectly planned-out life to God, and in doing so, I want Him to write my story; this book is a part of that surrender. I want to share the sweet places I have met with Jesus and what He has taught me about myself, about Him, and His will. Learning hasn't come easy, and these lessons don't automatically come to mind daily, but I recognize my responsibility in looking for Jesus in my desert. And as I sit here writing, the Lord reveals that the first command in Genesis 1:28 isn't "to multiply" but to "be fruitful," and there is so much fruit, my sweet sisters! A season of waiting on answers doesn't need to be a fruitless season.

Years ago, I was speaking with a terminally ill friend who asked me why God was testing her with her disease. We'd become very close, and our conversations often were about death, the afterlife, and her experience. Usually, I would only listen because I had nothing relatable to add, and I was always humbly struck by her candidness, but that day I felt overwhelmingly prompted to rephrase the question she posed out loud about being tested. I said, "What if He isn't testing you but trusting you?" And as her life came to an end over the next few months, I witnessed her share the love of the Lord with everyone she came across. I regularly think back to this conversation to recalibrate how I choose to show up in situations. How will I represent the Lord? What if this is an invitation to trust Him? John 15:5 states, "I am the vine; you are the branches. If you remain in me and I in you, you will bear much fruit; apart from me, you can do nothing."

- Where do you see Jesus on your journey?

- Have you learned something new that could only come from God and because of struggling with infertility?

- What would laying your diagnosis at Jesus's feet mean?

On a related note: I have a friend who had multiple miscarriages while trying to conceive and now has two children. She experienced the same feelings and thoughts about the lack of appreciation she thought other women had as moms. We've talked at length about the guilt she struggles with because now she gets frustrated and overwhelmed with motherhood. Please don't do this to yourself. Some women who are reading this will eventually get pregnant and go through similar stages. The truth is the grass is always greener on the other side. Until we are in those shoes, we will never understand. And the same goes for people who have not dealt with infertility. Let's focus on extending grace, not judgment. Grace is acknowledging we're all in process. Judgment is viewing the world through a lens of critical, uninformed opinions. Let's empower and encourage to the absolute best of our ability and leave the rest to God. Ladies, the world asks so much of us already; let's help each other through life, celebrating our wins and mourning our losses rather than condemning our choices and comparing our lives.

Rest

I can't think of a struggle I've faced that my relationship with God and my faith in Him hasn't overcome. We've always come out on the other side of a problem relatively quickly, hand in hand. Infertility is a beast among beasts, and it's challenged my faith on the most personal level, calling out my character, uprooting untruths in my belief system and my capacity to trust the Lord. My mind understands God has plans in store for my husband and me; my mouth says it, but my heart doubts it. Ultimately, I've come to acknowledge my doubt stems from fear God won't fix our circumstances the way I want.

At first, I felt like I had to infuse positivity and hope into our story when all I really felt like doing was shutting myself away to sit in my grief. To this day, I struggle with the people-pleasing pressure of reassuring others when they find out we can't have biological children. I rush to tell them how grateful we are to be an aunt and uncle and joke about how thankful I am that we can sleep in uninterrupted, all to ease the tension, narrowly avoiding potential awkwardness or unwanted advice. The constant offense-defense strategy makes an already difficult situation utterly draining.

I've gone through life as a happy, optimistic, early riser (yep, I'm one of those girls), trying to live my life as stress-free, simple, and authentically as possible. I've grappled with an overwhelming feeling of self-hatred as I clumsily navigate the world of infertility. I feel trapped in this vicious circle of emotions.

The deep sadness I walk around with because of our situation breeds an insidious hopelessness fueling anger and envy toward others who don't have to deal with infertility. Then I cycle into becoming frustrated and embarrassed how often these feelings happen, making me resent my own self because of all these negative feelings I have. Then along comes guilt because "I don't want to be this person," a person who covets what others have, a person who worries her faith is tied more into her own plan than God's. This nightmare emotional merry-go-round is endless and exhausting. Not only do I have to confront our circumstances, but now I also have to grapple with my character.

I created a strict workout routine, scheduled private clients, and socially packed my calendar with dinners, events, and coffee dates. For the longest time, I was drowning as I tried to keep my head above water from the busyness I created in a misguided effort to ignore how I was feeling. As God does, He spoke to me through a sermon series our pastor was teaching about spiritual discipline. Spiritual disciplines like prayer, tithing, or regularly reading the Bible are practices purposefully followed to grow and strengthen our relationship with God. The pastor challenged the congregation to set aside time to participate in the discipline of Sabbath rest. Ideally, it would be a whole day of rest, but if an entire day weren't an option, a few consecutive hours to recharge would make a difference. Honestly, the idea of rest sounded necessary because the pace I had set intentionally overbooking myself was bordering on punishment.

The first mention of the Sabbath in the Bible is in Exodus, chapter 16. Before coming to this conversation between Moses and the Israelites, a little background is needed. The Israelites were under Egyptian oppression, but with Moses's obedience and God's grace, they freed them to journey east toward Jericho. Before their journey, they witnessed God's plagues on Egypt; during their forty-year trek, God "went before them by day in a pillar of cloud to lead the way, and by night in a pillar of fire to give them light" (Exod. 13:21). The Israelites boldly walked through the division of the Red Sea (Exod. 14), drank the sweet water of Marah eagerly after God had Moses throw a piece of wood into the bitter lake (Exod. 15:22–25), and ate manna God provided from heaven (Exod. 16). To say they had plenty of reasons to trust and fear God is an understatement; however, their doubt and potential discomfort gave Moses a run for his money.

We pick up on their travels at the "Wilderness of Sin, which is between Elim and Sinai, on the fifteenth day of the second month after they departed from the land of Egypt" (Exod. 16:1). I want to point out the Israelites deserve some major credit for their courage. Despite my annoyance at their frequent grumbling, they've been walking a long time into an unknown land, unknown circumstances, in an unknown direction, and I can relate to that right now. Trusting God is deeply uncomfortable for me, not because He isn't faithful, but because even the illusion of control is gone when I step out in faith. The Israelites were more comfortable with the familiar, brutal treatment of the Egyptians than the liberating freedom God wanted for them in exchange for their trust.

Infertility is a rare road, pitted with fear: Will God bless us with children? How can I prepare my heart for the fight ahead if He leads us into the foster care system? When my thoughts become all jumbled up with plans, options, and fears, I get overwhelmed, anxious, bad-tempered, and, dare I say it, complain-y. Hello, Pot; meet Kettle. Ouch. I have the attitude of the Israelites when I trust solely in myself and my abilities. God designed feelings, making them perfectly normal, and my habit of compartmentalizing them into good or bad concepts forms the trajectory of my experience with them. I was working overtime, running from hard, unpleasant feelings, choosing not to invite God to help me safely explore them.

Going back to the Israelites in the Wilderness of Sin: they grew hungry at their arrival. They complained to Moses and Aaron that, although they would've died at the Egyptians' hands, at least they had food and were full (Exod. 16:2, 3). God answered that He would rain bread from heaven, and the Israelites were to gather a quota that met the needs of each person, but on the sixth day, they were to gather twice as much. On the seventh day, they could rest without worry.

> This is what the Lord has said: "Tomorrow is a Sabbath rest, a holy Sabbath to the Lord. Bake what you will bake today, and boil what you will boil; and lay up for yourselves all that remains, to be kept until morning." So they laid it up till the morning, as Moses commanded, and it did not stink, nor were there any worms in it. Then Moses said, "Eat that today, for today is a Sabbath to the Lord; today you will not find it in the field. Six days you shall gather it, but on the seventh day, the Sabbath, there will be none." (Exod. 16:23–26 NIV)

God chose to fullfill a physcial need for the weary Israelites as well as a need harder to identify-rest.

God is giving the weary Israelites the gift of food and the revitalizing opportunity to rest: "[W]hen the layer of dew lifted, there, on the surface of the wilderness, was a small, round substance, as fine as frost on the ground" (16:14) and "It was like white coriander seed, and the taste of it was like wafers made with honey" (16:31).

On my first attempt at Sabbath, I realized that it was a time I would have to fight to follow through. I lasted about four hours, all the while fielding text messages about keeping my mom company as she ran errands, and a patient who never reached out to me outside of office hours was in a great deal of pain and needed myofascial release. Sitting in that unfamiliar, awkward quiet, I desperately wanted to say yes to my mom, and not being productive was making me feel antsy. I ended up going to my patient's house to give them a massage therapy treatment. I figured, Wouldn't God want me to help?

I knew deep in my soul God had been calling me to sit with Him and talk all my feelings out, but I was avoiding Him. He has bigger fish to fry, right? I have a lot to be grateful for, so why should I go to the Creator of the universe and ask Him for one more thing? Truthfully, I was afraid of how He would answer. I was fearful of showing Him the person I'd become. I worried if I became vulnerable, if I put on display for Him the inky blackness that had become me, I would break.

Let's jump back and see how the Israelites responded: "Now it happened that some of the people went out on the seventh day to gather, but they found none" (Exod. 16:29). Fail. They didn't do so hot. I understand it on a human level: the fear, the need for control, the "Are you sure that's what you mean, God?" hesitation. Look at my attempt on my first Sabbath; I only lasted a handful of hours!

Waiting for His answers can seem incredibly inconvenient; we live in a world of instant gratification and daily demands, where waiting doesn't feel like an option. However, in this paused place, I remember this is the Creator of the universe who chose to call me Daughter. In His Fatherly wisdom, He answers me with what I need to grow. Generally speaking, I find His timing and answers aren't only about resolution, but also more focused on maturing me for my benefit.

"Wait" is a response from the Lord and a call to action on our end. Participating in a Sabbath rest deliberately makes space for Him to speak, me to hear, and the opportunity to absorb and reflect on what He says. In today's world, the speed at which we live our lives doesn't leave room for rest; instead, we become convinced rest is unnecessary, a by-product of the lazy and unsuccessful. This belief is embedded in the current rhythm of our society, distracting us, making us weary, anxious, and overwhelmed.

Dedicating time to the Lord serves to improve the discipline of listening prepares my heart for accepting His answers and obeying His call. In my personal experience, as the Lord responds to my prayers, there is responsibility I have to follow through with whatever He's placed on my heart. I have heard the Lord say, "Wait, but while you wait, share my love to the hurting."

Round two. The following week I scheduled a Sabbath for myself on Saturday. All week I prepared myself, my husband, and my family that my goal was to honor my Sabbath time by staying at home. I set aside a book I wanted to finish, kept my journal close by, and hunkered into bed. A sweet sister in Christ gifted me *Present Over Perfect*, by Shauna Niequist, a book about her journey back to simplicity, connection, and acceptance. Her writing enveloped me as if I were sitting with a girlfriend having one of those rare, heartfelt talks.

Not far from where I started reading, she writes:

> In some moments, I feel such profound self-hatred, and that terrible darkness bleeds out onto everything around me, the way darkness does. I could recognize it as separate from me, not built on the true materials of my life or circumstances, but more like a curtain dropping, like a virus infecting everything. It became harder and harder to walk well on those days…it became more visible once I slowed down a little. Maybe it's part of the reason I'd been running. (67)

I began to cry, a guttural release. I can unequivocally relate to what Shauna Niequist wrote, and I had so much shame for feeling this way. I'm a daughter of the almighty God and have been a believer since junior high, yet here I was doubting, scared, letting Him down, my husband and my family down, and I couldn't fix it. I couldn't work my way back to happiness. That darkness had seeped into my relationships. I had become hypercritical of my husband, impatient with my family, and emotionally exhausted at work, and worst of all, I was burning myself out with busyness to avoid God.

I whipped out my journal and began to write all the nasty, vile things I had witnessed about my character since struggling with infertility. All the emotions I thought I was above. You'd think that wouldn't have been a real confidence booster, and initially, it wasn't, but then I heard a whisper: "I love you. I love you for who you are. I love you in this, because of it, despite it, and for it." God was speaking, and I had slowed down enough to sit and examine these feelings and recognize the lies the enemy was feeding me. If anyone else had described what I was going through, I would instantly have validated their feelings and encouraged them to treat themselves gently in their cruel judgment. And isn't it true that we judge ourselves more harshly?

I also realized I needed to invite God into my anguish instead of traveling alone. I was able to admit to my husband that this darkness was affecting my life, and I believed I was struggling with depression and needed a healthy outlet through counseling. Sabbath helped me become fully aware of how I grew weary and bitter in an effort to ignore. I desperately needed to break the cycle. My feelings, your feelings, deserve the courtesy of being acknowledged. Our grief has a purpose. Right now, it feels like it just sets up shop to remind us of our heartbreak relentlessly, but we can take ownership and turn it to our advantage. We can experience our grief, explore it so that we can heal. God sees my hurt, and He holds my healing. I'm choosing to work through this and get back to loving life again, embracing my path, enjoying the company around me, and most importantly, loving myself again.

The rest of that Sabbath I spent cuddling on the couch with Mike and watching TV. It was healing to be held and to relax. Rest does that. It refills your cup. It redirects you. You can't continue to give without receiving. We fall victim to the deception that choosing you is selfish. You have to take care of yourself before you can adequately take care of others. If there is anything that I pray you take away from my journey, it is this: self-care and being selfish are not the same thing. If anyone tells you differently, reflect on why they might be saying that: their lack of care in their life, motives, and where they fit in your support system.

One of the things I'm excited about as I write this is that I won't have my end-of-the-tunnel type answer when it's finished. I just have the truths I know today. I'm still working on what Sabbath looks like to me. Emotionally, in this second, I'm doing good. Tomorrow may be different, and I'll roll with it through prayer and support.

- Are you resting?

- How can you incorporate self-care this week?

- Do you feel like you may need professional help to sort out your feelings?

Anger

I had always believed grief to be associated with the death of a loved one and nothing else. Throughout life, I've come to understand that grief is a process that occurs organically through various circumstances: in dreams left unaccomplished, in the breakdown of a relationship, or sitting in a doctor's office after a diagnosis. It's where we wrestle with our expectations and preconceived ideas, let go of what we knew or wanted, and acknowledge the reality in front of us. I once heard grief described as the opposite of dreaming and the absolution of hope. My grief experience felt dark and isolating; despite having family and friends surrounding me, I felt utterly alone, which I would argue is truly the loneliest.

Grief is widely taught to have five stages: denial, anger, bargaining, depression, and acceptance, the Kübler-Ross model. However, there has been some criticism on how this process is understood and taught in the psychology world. Even the theorist herself, Elizabeth Kübler-Ross, noted that the stages are not linear with predictable progression, and she regretted writing them in a way that was misunderstood: "'Kübler-Ross originally saw these stages as reflecting how people cope with illness and dying,' observed grief researcher Kenneth J. Doka, 'not as reflections of how people grieve.'"

Sounds silly to say I have a favorite stage, not because I enjoy it, but because I am so familiar with it. Anger. Denial was a slow fade when it came to our infertility because the diagnosis was an extensive process, and there seemed to be relatively plenty of treatment options. Eventually, ignoring the truth behind our diagnosis became less easy, but when I reached this juncture, I'd been through enough testing and appointments; reality was full-body-slamming me like a professional hockey player with a temper problem. Those dudes can be vicious, right?

Anger, on the other hand, comes burning in like a raging wildfire, vengeful and fierce. "What did we do wrong? Why us and not them?" ("Them" typically being people you read about who do horrible, indescribable things to their kids.) But let's be honest; sometimes we can ask the same question about people closest to us. "Why won't you bless us as you did them, God? How come you won't do a miracle here?"

Anger is an emotion I am comfortable with and willingly accept. I was exceptionally good at reveling in its all-consuming presence, using it as fuel to motivate me. I would feed off being angry, hold grudges, and fantasize about my well-formed words of retaliation. Anger was my default emotion, one I eventually came to realize was a cover-up for other, more deeply rooted feelings I didn't want to explore. Anger makes us defensive, creating division between our hearts, people in our lives, and God if we don't confront the reasons behind its presence.

First, our infertility isn't a punishment. Satan uses this concept as a weapon to cultivate distrust of our Father. Satan uses insecurities from our past to shape our circumstances into consequences, making us believe we deserve to go through infertility. Wrong. Infertility may be our reality, but it has no connection with sin in our life, past or present. John 9:1–3 addresses this thought process outright: "As [Jesus] went along, he saw a man blind from birth. His disciples asked him, 'Rabbi, who sinned, this man or his parents, that he was born blind?' 'Neither this man nor his parents sinned,' said Jesus, 'but this happened so that the works of God might be displayed in him.'"

Rather than being concerned with the why or placing blame, Jesus changes the tone of the conversation. He redirects the disciples' focus to the purpose. Jesus was already looking forward to the fruit that would develop through the situation, whereas the disciples were hung up on trying to fit this man's blindness into an earthly perspective. Stop now and imagine Jesus saying to you, "This happened so that the works of God might be displayed in you."

And yes, I hear you out there, you Bible aficionado: "What about David and Bethsheba's son in Second Samuel 12?" God did indeed take the life of their firstborn because of David's sin—having sex with Bethsheba and having her husband, Uriah, killed. I can't answer why God chose to have the young boy die of illness due to David's sin, but I can tell you how incredibly sad it made me. Sorry for the death of a young boy, sad for the parents, and sad because sin sucks. Sin is a destroyer that eagerly corrupts lives, damages relationships, produces division, and robs people of their peace. I will not defend or condemn God's actions because I only have a human outlook, nor is it my place, but I am placing His response in perspective. Ultimately, we have to examine our hearts and look at the characteristics of God. God has been faithful, loving, gentle, and patient in my life, and knowing that about God reaffirms that infertility is not a punishment.

Over time I have learned anger is an indicator of a deeper issue, not a tool I should use to influence or excuse my actions. Redirecting my anger does nothing, but when I choose to acknowledge it, rooting out the other emotions beneath so I can learn how to heal is the ultimate resolution. To that point, healing is a choice. We don't choose trauma or hardships, but we do choose how we deal with them. Confronting adversity isn't easy, but neither is avoiding it. Burying and evading the hurt can manifest itself physically with illness, affect relationships caused by emotional indifference and disengagement, and ultimately create more suffering.

Taking the possibility this was a punishment off the table, my defensive anger that developed out of hurt changed. I was still angry, though. This time I felt righteous in my anger, and this is where I want to focus. My human definition of righteousness versus God's definition is entirely different. For me, bringing God my heart raw from sadness was more manageable than bringing Him my heart that had turned indignant. Mike and I don't deserve infertility. We'd be loving and fun parents who have a strong marriage! I felt mistreated and felt that God was unjust.

When my heart was busy being resentful, it didn't leave time for these new feelings to be compared to my list of characteristics of the God I know so well. These were the moments where sin entered my story. God calls us to "get rid of all bitterness, rage, and anger, brawling and slander, along with every form of malice" (Eph. 4:31). When I choose to hang on to my anger, it defies God and places barriers between me and God's purpose. Anger was interfering with my ability to grieve because it helped me avoid the pain, preventing an open, honest conversation with God and falsely teaching me vulnerability is a weakness.

Mike and I have been reading through the Bible this year, and Moses is a man who shows up early, and you quickly become invested in his story. Moses's birth is recorded in Exodus 2, along with his mother's brave decision to trust God, sending him in a basket down the Nile to escape murder. Moses is found, raised in Pharaoh's household, and kills an Egyptian for beating a Hebrew, then goes on the run. He becomes a shepherd and has an encounter with God at a burning bush. God calls Moses to lead His people out of Egypt and into freedom from their oppressors. He ministers to these people for forty years, right up to the land God promised. This is seriously the most condensed version you will ever get. Throughout this adventure, Moses was a man with a mighty trust in God, doing all that was asked of him and leading people that were nothing short of a challenge.

The Israelites were easily swayed throughout the journey. In Exodus 16, they're found complaining about not having meat to eat; in chapter 32, we find that while Moses is receiving the Ten Commandments on Mount Sinai, the Israelites build a golden calf to worship. In Numbers 11, we find them complaining again about their lack of food options. I'm pretty sure I wouldn't have had the patience for that if I were Moses. Moses goes to God each time the mob becomes angry and entitled, knowing he isn't in charge of the provisions or the consequences.

This brings us to Numbers 20:1–12:

> The people of Israel arrived at the Zin Desert during the first month and set up camp near the town of Kadesh. It was there that Miriam died and was buried. The Israelites had no water, so they went to Moses and Aaron and complained, "Moses, we'd be better off if we had died along with the others in front of the Lord's sacred tent. You brought us into this desert, and now we and our livestock are going to die! Egypt was better than this horrible place. At least there, we had grain and figs and grapevines and pomegranates. But now we don't even have any water." Moses and Aaron went to the entrance of the sacred tent, where they bowed down. The Lord appeared to them in all of His glory and said, "Moses, get your walking stick. Then you and Aaron

call the people together and command that rock to give you water. That's how you will provide water for the people of Israel and their livestock." Moses obeyed and took his stick from the sacred tent. After he and Aaron had gathered the people around the rock, he said, "Look, you rebellious people, and you will see water flow from this rock!" He raised his stick in the air and struck the rock two times. Water gushed from the rock at once, and the people and their livestock had water to drink. But the Lord said to Moses and Aaron, "Because you refused to believe in My power, these people did not respect Me. And so, you will not be the ones to lead them into the land I have promised."

Moses lost his composure, causing him to lose sight of God. God instructed Moses to speak to the rock, whereas Moses smacked it with his staff twice. I imagine a tired, frustrated Moses standing in front of the Israelites at his boiling point, caused by their constant complaining, and striking the rock with a sudden, violent movement, Moses's action stunning the crowd as the sound reverberates off the walls of the canyon.

I remember once Mike and I were talking through a personal issue, and I became enraged, throwing a paper towel roll I had been holding, as hard as I could, at the wall, surprising both myself and Mike. I witnessed explosive, unpredictable anger as a kid, and I knew I desperately didn't want to repeat the same behavior because I recall the fear it produced. If someone could allow their anger to drive their actions and words so impulsively, what else were they physically capable of? I was embarrassed Mike had seen me lash out, but even more so, I was ashamed. I threw an adult-sized tantrum, letting anger dictate my actions instead of pausing and having honesty lead us to a productive discussion. What was done was done, though, and in that split second, as I threw the paper towels, I thought my action and anger were justifiably reasonable.

In actuality, I have control over my actions, and I have the opportunity to either react in response to how I am feeling in the moment or pause, collect my thoughts, and respond in a more articulated way. Feelings aren't fact, and allowing them to be the primary influence on how I respond leaves room for unnecessary problems. I often find myself mentally molding situations in life as proof to validate my feelings, and in the work of infertility, it's important to be proactive instead of reactive.

Going back to Moses, we see that his action was a reaction. He let his anger guide him instead. His response disrespected God and had heavy consequences. Moses would not be allowed to enter the promised land.

I don't want the anger infertility has created to define me or our situation. I won't allow the anger to lead my emotions to a place where contempt builds a stronghold on my heart. I choose to explore my anger and ask questions that will bring me through it:

1. Is there a belief behind my anger I need to face?

2. Is anger covering up an emotion I am avoiding?

3. Have I created a pattern of sin in my life because of the anger I am feeling?

I wouldn't be here learning and growing if I wasn't struggling with infertility. One of the things I have been undeniably made aware of during this time in my life is how much God is remolding me, shaping a future I hadn't had the capacity to dream about. I have been purposeful in refusing to let an already complicated situation be bogged down with the ramifications of sin.

The mystery of the Lord, the beauty of the Lord, is that His judgment is interconnected to His mercy. Without judgment, we wouldn't know where we stand with God, therefore missing the opportunity for repentance. I find repentance is the space where I gain maturity. Even though it's difficult and incredibly uncomfortable, I'm thankful God loves me so much He roots out the sin that has destructive potential. God is refining my faith and redeeming my story through this season because He is a loving Father. Moses's story doesn't end with the Lord's judgment being handed to him but with the love of the Lord surrounding him:

> Then Moses climbed Mount Nebo from the plains of Moab to the top of Pisgah, across from Jericho. There the Lord showed

him the whole land—from Gilead to Dan, all of Naphtali, the territory of Ephraim and Manasseh, all the land of Judah as far as the Mediterranean Sea, the Negev and the whole region from the Valley of Jericho, the City of Palms, as far as Zoar. Then the Lord said to him, "This is the land I promised on oath to Abraham, Isaac, and Jacob when I said, 'I will give it to your descendants.' I have let you see it with your eyes, but you will not cross over into It." And Moses the servant of the Lord died there in Moab, as the Lord had said. He buried him in Moab, in the valley opposite Beth Peor, but to this day no one knows where his grave is. (Deut. 34:1–6 NIV)

Here's the beauty of Moses's story: yes, God as a Father had to follow through with the consequences He gave him, but He still loved, respected, and cared for Moses. He gave Moses the gift of seeing the land. I picture Moses on this mountainside, watching the most stunning sunset, wrapped up in God's presence like the comfiest of blankets, reveling in the peace of completing his mission for God, humbled at the provisions and mighty power God provided through the journey, and resting like he never rested before. Did you catch what God did at the end in verse 6? He buried Moses. He took the time and care to lovingly place Moses's body respectfully in the ground and never left him. Writing this, I am in tears at the love the

Father shows. We can screw up. We can grow distant, react poorly, or struggle with trust, but none of that changes our Father's deep love for you and me. We will always be the Lord's treasure.

- Do you wrestle with feeling justifiably angry?

- What could potentially happen if you held on to your anger?

- Is holding on a better option than giving it to God?

On a different note: Righteous anger defined by humans is contrary to the genuine righteous anger of God. In Matthew 21:12–13, we see Jesus at the temple courts, driving out all who were buying and selling doves because the focus on faith had been lost and replaced with greed. The place meant for sacred worship had turned into "a den of robbers." The concern was no longer for the people but business. True righteous anger is being passionate about the things that make God angry—corrupting His goodness and the exploitation of His glory. My "righteous" heart was created by resentment, closing me off from God. Precisely what Satan wanted, and he is incredibly subtle at taking content out of context. We can't see the bigger picture; all we have is this narrow lens. Infertility can make us extremely vulnerable to Satan's lies. Guarding our hearts has to be our priority; we can't take our eyes off God. Otherwise, just like Peter in Matthew 14:22–32, we will sink.

Seen

A few weeks ago, Karen, a dear friend of mine, came to visit me at work. I first met her professionally, and we quickly developed a friendship based on our common wit, love of music, and mutual joy in our conversations. I watched her family go through indescribable heartache, overcome adversity most of us will never face, and celebrate wonderfully sweet moments. Her direct honesty and abundant knowledge continue to help me endure the struggles of infertility to this day. During her visit, she gave me an unexpected gift. Upon opening the box, I saw a simple, round, silver necklace with an arrow etched in the center and a card that read, "An arrow has to go backward to go forward." I looked up, and Karen said to me, "I got you this gift because I see you. I know you're struggling, and when I saw this necklace, it made me think of you." That moment still brings tears to my eyes because I felt invisible, painfully lonely, and forgotten. Karen will never know just how perfect her timing was and how the sincerity of her heart and words gave me the support I desperately needed.

The first year after our diagnosis was overwhelmingly emotional and incredibly exhausting. The sorrow I felt dominated my thoughts, stealing all my energy. Most days, I didn't have the fortitude to find God in our situation because I was too busy trying to act as if I were unaffected, which only worked about a third of the time. I immediately understood grief made people (and me) uncomfortable, so I spent a lot of time trying to avoid being honest with myself about the depression I was undergoing or coming to the rescue of those around me, reassuring them that I was OK.

Infertility had a cruel way of making Mike and me feel isolated, insignificant, brushed aside, and left behind, as people moved forward with their lives while we were haphazardly picking up the pieces of ours. I began to feel abandoned by God, especially when we had more questions than answers or when my heart felt like it would physically split from heartache. Eventually, when I listened to God's call to rest, I realized God wasn't absent but that I had pushed Him aside, creating a raw, exposed space. I was responsible for the separation between Him and me, allowing room for the lie to take root that God didn't see my broken heart.

God sees me, and He sees you. As I survey the last few years and all God has lovingly taught me through infertility, I see He is pulling the arrow back, clearing out the distorted beliefs that have crept into my faith, so I can go forward. If God didn't see me, He wouldn't take the time to uproot what shouldn't be there. After confronting the lie turned into belief, "God didn't see me," I had to go a step further and evaluate why that lie gained the momentum it had. I didn't have to go very far. In being honest with myself, I was frustrated that I did "all the right things" and God wouldn't answer my prayer to become pregnant.

There is no easy way to write this: I believed that God would miraculously make us conceive if I was a "good enough" Christian. I was proud of how I'd grown in my faith, turning the fruit of it into a standardized checklist:

1. Go to church.

2. Repent of sin.

3. Volunteer.

4. Share my faith with others.

5. Cooperate in Spirit-led conflict resolution.

In my mind, if the above checklist was met, God would give me what I wanted, and since He hadn't, He clearly didn't care or was too busy for me. In actuality, the rules I created tainted the unadulterated grace of the Gospel and devalued Jesus's gift of connection. Imposing a merit-based system on myself led to the expectation that God's favor was inextricably linked to our infertility.

Scripture radically paints a different picture. In Acts 15, Paul, Barnabas, and Peter are standing before elders in Jerusalem debating whether the Gentile believers should be circumcised according to Israelite law and tradition:

> After there had been much debate, Peter stood up and said to them, "My brothers, you know that in the early days God made a choice among you, that I should be the one through whom the Gentiles would hear the message of the good news and become believers. And God, who knows the human heart, testified to them by giving them the Holy Spirit, just as He did to us; and in cleansing their hearts by faith, He has made no distinction between them and us. Now, therefore, why are you putting God to the test by placing on the neck of the disciples a yoke that neither our ancestors nor we have been able to bear? On the contrary, we believe that we will be saved through the grace of the Lord Jesus, just as they will." (Acts 15:7–11 NIV)

The early Jewish believers wanted the Gentiles to abide by laws that they couldn't and wouldn't follow and that Jesus's life and death removed the need for. The Bible is eminently clear that works are not associated with our salvation, and the harm of creating standards or trying to reach a form of perfection (which I have learned is usually unattainable or unsustainable) diverts us from the true purpose of our faith. I would never look at another person and tell them that in order to receive God's attention, they would have to participate in my checklist or someone else's. This thought process is damaging and has the potential to lead people to have more faith in themselves and their definition of "righteousness," creating a narrative where our actions and checklists give us an arrogant illusion we earned our place before God, when, in fact, a relationship with Jesus is the only way to God. In Luke 18:10–14, Jesus shares a parable showing us exactly how God deals with self-righteousness:

> "Two men went up to the temple to pray, one a Pharisee and the other a tax collector. The Pharisee stood by himself and prayed: 'God, I thank you that I am not like other people—robbers, evildoers, adulterers—or even like this tax collector. I fast twice a week and give a tenth of all I get.' But the tax collector stood at a distance. He would not look up to heaven, but beat his breast and said, 'God, have mercy on me, a sinner.' I tell you that this man, rather than the other, went home justified before God. For all those who exalt themselves will be humbled, and those who humble themselves will be exalted."

Placing requirements on our faith journey takes the need for a relationship with Christ away. Could you imagine having a set of ever-changing guidelines, designed by another person, you had to follow solely to please God? How unfair, arbitrary, and unachievable would that make living a faith-based life? I did that to myself! Why?

I am an action-driven person who strives for the elusively unattainable concept of perfection. I have lived life believing the effort you put in directly affects the outcome you want to see. Checklists create order and sense where grace and rest are harder concepts to grasp. So difficult, in fact, that instead of scrapping the checklist, I decided it must not be complete. Around this same time, I was being convicted to tithe. Tithing is an act of worship I struggle with because I place my security in money. When Mike and I were first married, I remember worrying about how we would pay for an unplanned bill. I would constantly pray that we wouldn't get sick or hurt since we didn't have health insurance, making a trip to the doctor or emergency room a debt-filled fear. By God's grace and wisdom, we are in a place now where we get a bill and automatically pay it off without concern.

However, fear had taken hold, creating a worry that we may not have enough money again one day. Without inviting Mike into the decision, I developed a strict spending policy we maintained for a year to reach a ten-thousand-dollar goal. Whenever we spent money on what I considered frivolous or unnecessary, like an ice cream trip to Culver's on a hot summer day, I obsessively stressed over how that eight bucks could've been placed into our savings instead. Needless to say, although saving is an important, godly principle, it had become an unhealthy focus in my life.

On the day I could not manage to explain, argue, or defend my way out of not tithing, I was visiting my mom. Yelling, I told her about God calling me to tithe. I burst into tears, upset at how this act of worship would limit what we could save each month. How could God ask me to trust Him with one more thing? How could He want more from me at a time like this? Why, during the toughest season of my life, would He weed out another one of my faults?

My reaction to God's calling was less than awesome, but soon, my resentful attitude turned into the idea that maybe tithing would be the ticket! This was the missing point on the checklist, and if Mike and I were faithful, God would let us get pregnant! That did not happen. First, I learned that acts of worship might have to start as a discipline. Initially, I began to tithe because it was something I was being called to do, not understanding why it was important; however, through the process, the hold money had over me was breaking. I began to see that it wasn't up to me to provide; it was God's. God gave me work, which gave me a roof over my head, which gave me food and money to pay bills. I wanted to give back to Him because I was thankful for His provision and all He has given to me—giving made me more grateful, opening my eyes to my many blessings. In a season where jealousy sprouted up feverishly quickly and unwanted, looking at what I had to be thankful for was a simple salve to ease the pain.

I'm starting to recognize the convoluted ideas I carry around and how they shape the image of my Father and my faith in my heart. Sometimes our lack of trust in Him is because we don't understand who He is. These lies make the foundation of my faith "like a person who builds a house on sand. When the rains and floods come, and the winds beat against that house, it will collapse with a mighty crash" (Matt. 7:26–27). Through infertility, God has rebuilt my house, taking down the warped support beams and replacing them with a solid and stable framework. What we do with our thoughts and actions is evidence of Jesus.

I find it challenging not to get swallowed up in the details of life when it feels like it's falling to pieces. Allowing God to see me has been sort of like spring cleaning with the freshness only truth can bring. Soon the pieces of my life that felt as if they were haphazardly falling, felt more like they were shifting into place.

- Have you invited God into your circumstances?

- Have you talked to Him honestly about how you're feeling?

- Do you have unfounded beliefs about God?

Side note: If you are reading this because you have someone in your life who is dealing with infertility and you're at a loss on how to support them, here are a few suggestions:

1. Ask them directly how you can support them.

2. If you think a day may be a hard one (Mother's Day, a gender reveal, the anniversary of a miscarriage, baby shower, or birth), a quick text or phone call asking how they are goes a long way.

Listen, giving them the freedom to say all that's on their heart and mind without judgment or giving advice (unless they specifically ask). My sister Nicole and my Uncle Jerry did this all the time, especially when my twin sister was pregnant. They made a difference in my life, reminding me that I was important and loved. They showed me you can still celebrate with others while coming alongside those who are hurting.

I have been on the other side of the fence, watching people I love hurt and struggling with feeling completely powerless. We can let our worry of being inadequate jam us up altogether. We become paralyzed for fear of not saying the right thing, being worried we aren't doing enough or that we will remind our loved one of their hurts if we say anything. Trust me when I tell you: knowing you see us—our sadness, our empty arms, our brave faces—and then letting us know you are here truly is the best gift.

Side note two: I can't describe how liberating it is to realize I should and can ditch my Christian criteria checklist. Who doesn't want one less thing to worry about, right? The creation of this list does me no good and has no benefits. I want to give you other verses to explore that support the fundamental principle that our works cannot save us. Loving God "with all your heart and with all your soul and with all your strength" is our focus as believers. Any good and excellent thing that comes from us is the fruit of the relationship we have with our Creator!

Titus 3:5, Acts 4:12, Romans 3:27–28, 2 Corinthians 1:9, John 6:28–29, James 2:10–11

Share
(The Eve Effect)

I have a terrible habit that I justify with excuses. I choose to go through hard times alone. My choice has nothing to do with not having people who are willing to come around and support me. I make my choice based on the worry I'll be bothering someone with my problems. I disengage from my people—husband, family, friends, and sisters in Christ—because "I should be able to handle it on my own; they've got so much going on;" or "They've already heard my story…" I have had a lifetime convincing myself these are legitimately reasonable rationales. Adding insult to injury, I have gone as far as persuading myself that my family and friends would 100 percent agree with this type of reasoning!

In this season, however, I'm learning about the subtlety of Satan. Satan is good at coming across as sensible and appealing to my nature. God has given me the gift of encouragement. It's an action I do naturally and with ease. I love building people up when they're having a hard day, I long to comfort people who are grieving, and I acknowledge people battling with self-esteem issues, and because of that, I have succumbed to the lie that if I invite someone into my sadness, my struggle, I'll bring them down. Instead, I purposefully alienate myself and go to battle alone, putting myself, my heart, and my mind in an incredibly vulnerable position.

When I think of a lady in a susceptible time in her life, I immediately remember our girl Eve. We don't have to go very far to find our first lady in a predicament, in Genesis 3:1–7:

> Now, the serpent was more crafty than any of the wild animals the Lord God had made. He said to the woman, "Did God really say, 'You must not eat from any tree in the garden?'" The woman said to the serpent, "We may eat fruit from the trees in the garden, but God did say, 'You must not eat fruit from the tree that is in the middle of the garden, and you must not touch it or you will surely die.'"
>
> "You will not surely die," the serpent said to the woman. "For God knows that when you eat of it your eyes will be opened, and you will be like God, knowing good and evil." When the woman saw that the fruit of the tree was good for food and pleasing

> to the eye, and also desirable for gaining wisdom, she took some and ate it. She also gave some to her husband, who was with her, and he ate it. Then the eyes of both of them were opened, and they realized they were naked; so they sewed fig leaves together and made coverings for themselves.

Every time I read this passage, I'm yelling, "*Stop!*" at the top of my lungs in my head. Can you imagine where we'd be if this never took place? Let's reread the passage again, but I'm going to insert the *stop* in my head onto the page.

> Now, the serpent was more crafty than any of the wild animals the Lord God had made. He said to the woman, "Did God really say, 'You must not eat from any tree in the garden?'" (*Stop!*) The woman said to the serpent, "We may eat fruit from the trees in the garden, but God did say, 'You must not eat fruit from the tree that is in the us middle of the garden, and you must not touch it (*Stop!*) or you will surely die.'"

> "You will not surely die," (*Stop!*) the serpent said to the woman. "For God knows that when you eat of it your eyes will be opened, and you will be like God, (*Stop!*) knowing good and evil." (*Stop!*) When the

woman saw that the fruit of the tree was good for food and pleasing to the eye, and also desirable for gaining wisdom, she took some (*Stop!*) and ate it. She also gave some to her husband, (*Stop!*) who was with her, and he ate it. Then the eyes of both of them were opened, and they realized they were naked; so they sewed fig leaves together and made coverings for themselves.

Let's see: that's seven stops, seven moments had God been invited into this moment He could have provided clarity and protection. Seven moments being alone counted against Eve. First, we know that the serpent has only addressed Eve and although later in the passage it says she "gave some to her husband who was with her," we aren't clear if Adam was with her the entire time the serpent was conversing with Eve. We know the snake deftly challenged God by changing His command from "You are free to eat from any tree in the garden, but you must not eat from the tree of knowledge of good and evil, for when you eat of it, you will surely die" to "You must not eat from any tree in the garden." I want Eve at this point to go, "You know, Mr. Serpent, I think that's more of a question for God, not me. He can correct your thinking way better than I can." She doesn't pick up on Satan's inaccurate version, but instead goes on to repeat what the Lord said and then includes, "And you must not touch it."

God never said that. Girl, don't be adding if you're unsure or lack even the slightest bit of confidence! Call out to God! Ask your husband to join you in this! The third *stop* solely has to do with just being frustrated; Eve is still entertaining the conversation with the serpent as he continues his deceitful conniving and convinces her she could be like God. Why would you want to be like God? Isn't He enough? Look around at this gorgeous, plentiful garden, Eve! Do you think you could do better? And why would you want to know evil? What benefit will that be to you, Eve? Take a look at what you do know: an intimate relationship with the Father and your husband, provision, and security. Sign me up! Although in all honesty, I admittedly concede to Satan at times too, believing I can defend myself without preparation or worse yet, allow him to speak into and inflate my insecurities.

As we continue, we find Eve reaching for the fruit and touching it without death, which is the piece she included during the conversation with the serpent. Her touching the fruit and not dying only benefits the serpent's earlier arguments. Then Eve takes a bite of the fruit and offers it to Adam.

Since the beginning of time, trusting God has evidently been a hard thing to do. Perhaps it's because we think we know better. Maybe we feel like God isn't paying attention, or He's moving too slowly for our liking. Whatever the reason, human nature inherently doubts God and grasps for control. We see plenty of examples in the Bible where people thought they knew better than God, only to wish they had listened to Him from the start.

Eve had walked with God in the garden, having all she truly needed for a sweetly fulfilling life. So do I. The

Lord of all creation desires to walk with me through life. An authentic relationship begins when I accept His initial invitation and then extend my own. Infertility can make me feel completely stranded. Satan can have the advantage by not allowing God, my husband, and my community into my grief. When I share my hard days, I give them and the emotions that come with them a little less power.

Tonight, I had a hard night. A friend delivered her baby, and instead of being joyful for her, I was jealous. I know that's normal and that after that emotional ride, I'll come to find joy for her. Earlier, I stewed in my jealousy, which turned into anger. I turned on praise music in my car, which tempered the sadness filling up my chest. I told my mom, who walks beside me, always prepared to listen and wipe my tears. I texted my friends Rachel and Nikki, who prayed with me immediately over the phone. I told Mike, who is endlessly watchful and sweet and takes my mood in stride.

Doing these things doesn't come easy because admitting to people that I am feeling angry and jealous of someone I love who is going through one of the most amazing moments of their lives makes me feel like a monster. And I am worried others will see me the same way. But I am not a monster, and neither are you. I don't want to feel envious or sad, but I do, and I need support as I work through it, which is why it's crucial to have people you can go to that you trust. Today was the first time I even texted Nikki, and all it said was, "Pray for me. I am having a hard day."

One of the other thoughts that crosses my mind about Eve's story is how often she thought of the moments she walked with God in the garden and what she should've done. If only she could do that day over, what her life would be like had she obeyed God, trusting that He had her best interest at heart. I don't want to be like Eve. I have the potential to let our situation make me bitter and resentful, and separate me from my Jesus, husband, family, and friends. When I choose to keep my tough days to myself, I create such distance between Mike and me, setting a mood in our home that can quickly cultivate insecurities. Having the confidence to share is only the first part. The second is knowing how to communicate:

> **1. Are you comfortable in the place you're at to share?** I am three years out from my diagnosis, and I still cry when sharing my story. I am used to having that reaction because it's normal, but I've learned crying at a Starbucks isn't my jam.
>
> **2. Are you placing your confidence in the right people?** Whom I choose to share with and what I choose to share with them is a privilege and not something that should be reshared or discussed elsewhere.
>
> **3. Understand you have the right to be direct.** If you're looking for someone to listen, without giving advice or an opinion, tell them! When I want someone to give me the grace of a listening ear, it's because I need to voice out loud the thoughts in my head. Some days you don't need a pep talk.

The reality is that God designed us for community: community with Him, with our husbands, and with our friends. We achieve more, love more, grow more, learn more as a community of believers. On a broader scope, consider the disciples and other believers in the days after Jesus was crucified, resurrected, and then taken up before their very eyes to be beside the Father. Acts 2:42–47 says:

> They devoted themselves to the apostles' teaching and to the fellowship, to the breaking of bread and to prayer. Everyone was filled with awe, and many wonders and miraculous signs were done by the apostles. All the believers were together and had everything in common. Selling their possessions and goods, they gave to anyone as he had need. Every day they continued to meet together in the temple courts. They broke bread in their homes and ate together with glad and sincere hearts, praising God and enjoying the favor of all the people. And the Lord added to their number daily those who were being saved.

Can you imagine if Peter, who denied Christ three times, had decided to split off from the group because he didn't feel worthy enough? What about the other early believers? How do you think their faith would have been nurtured if not for this community? They placed themselves in a position of dependence on one another by selling their things. They developed relationships around dinner tables. They worshipped together as they gathered in the temple courts. They did life together—the good and the bad. John 16:33 records Jesus saying, "In this world you will have trouble." It's a fact that just because we are believers in Christ does not mean we will be free from hard times. That makes me sure that although this description in Acts is a beautifully sweet picture of fellowship, there were hard times for people way back then. Maybe it was fear of the Sanhedrin (five chapters later, we find Stephen stoned by them); perhaps it's a disagreement at the dinner table, or a young woman unable to sing her praise and worship because her heart and arms are yearning for a baby. We do have to accept that we aren't immune to trials, but we do have the ability to share our heartaches with Jesus and, subsequently, our brothers and sisters in Christ.

Jesus follows up what He says in John 16:33 with: "But take heart! I have overcome the world." With this truth, Jesus is all that matters.

- Have you been closed off from your support group?

- Do you know who your support group is? Name three to five people you know you can call right now.

- Are you and your husband talking to and relying on each other?

- What reservations do you have about being honest with the people who love you?

- Can you see Satan's influence in trying to isolate you?

Boundaries

One of the most complex parts to navigate for me during the grief process has been boundaries. Guilt follows grief like a shadow I can't shake. Despite, or maybe even avoiding, my feelings, I place other people ahead of my own needs. When I choose to honor my emotions, a sense of responsibility toward others convicts me. I have experienced these feelings during events like baby showers and conversations that start with the harmless "When will you and Mike start your family?" tagline.

Baby showers…infertility and baby showers are tricky topics. For no rhyme or reason, I have been able to attend some and feel relaxed and entirely joyful, and at others, I have become heavyhearted and left emotionally exhausted. At this time of my life, invitations are pouring in left and right for baby showers, and with each one, I struggle with accepting the invitation. It is so much more than a yes or no on my availability that day. I go through the potential guest list in my mind for who might utter the "You're next," or even if someone is aware of our situation and may choose to hover with constant questions like "Are you OK?" I know it sounds terrible that innocent phrases have the potential to upset me, but when you struggle with infertility, protecting your heart comes with the territory, and to do that, you have to strategize. Then I think about how I might feel during the gift opening. Games and visiting don't bother me, but something about a tiny onesie can wreck my fragile heart.

Once while RSVPing to a shower, I felt the need to explain why I wasn't going to attend. Hello, guilt. The baby shower was going to be over my wedding anniversary weekend. Although I could attend, I recognized that I battled with envy during this friend's pregnancy, and the baby shower would make me uncomfortable. I didn't want any negative emotional influences over our celebratory weekend. Hello, wisdom. The host was aware of my diagnosis, and as we talked, I had said I wanted to make it clear I wasn't not coming due to my situation. I was worried it would be hurtful to my friend if she thought so. To my surprise, the young lady began to ask me why we had decided not to go through with IVF and gave her opinion on sperm donation, what she would do in our situation, the beauty of pregnancy, and what I was choosing to miss out on. I was stunned, hurt, and proud that I got off the phone without saying anything regretful. Her words made me feel like I didn't have the right to grieve because I hadn't tried everything medically available. She unknowingly put me in a position where I felt marginalized and like I had to defend my decision and my "right" to be heartbroken.

Here's what I've learned through multiple interactions like this one:

1. I don't owe an explanation to anyone, and if it is implied that I do, it's time for me to evaluate my relationship with them.

2. Respecting my emotional state is for the betterment of myself and others around me. My comfort is more important than their reality.

3. Practice makes progress. With time it truly becomes easier.

4. Habits and behavior are formed when rewarded. What you allow will continue.

These concepts are common sense but hard to practice because guilt rides in like a man on a mission. Guilt is a tool from Satan that we feel is interchangeable with conviction. Guilt is unproductive, a lie that prevents or inhibits us from learning from our experiences and relying on God. When I make decisions motivated by guilt, it's usually for something I feel like I have to power through. When I rely on my strength, I fail. I have learned a lot about guilt because Satan uses it as a weapon to his advantage. And when we are dealing with a lie, we have to look for truth, and the truth is Jesus's specialty.

I have two very special Bibles. One is purple and over fifteen years old; I bought it at a Women of Faith conference. That conference was a turning point for me because I realized then that faith requires trust, which leads to obedience, but trusting challenges my need for control. The weight of this book when I hold it feels like a homecoming each time. My second Bible is smaller and easier to carry, and it's my dad's. My dad and I are very similar in personality: funny, stubborn, motivated, and prideful. I cherish holding his Bible because his faith journey has been filled with curiosity, turbulence, and love. I want to remember his fight with grace because I connect to his struggle, so when I bought a new Bible, I traded mine for his. I love flipping through and seeing where he has highlighted, where he stopped to study and absorb truth. In this Bible, when Jesus speaks, it's written in red. The color red certainly grabs my attention; it screams, "Don't miss this! Take your time here!" Any time Jesus speaks, I want to use His words as a sifter and let anything else fall off.

In Matthew 5 we find Jesus teaching His disciples on a mountainside. Verse 37 records Him saying, "Simply let your 'yes' be a 'yes' and your 'no,' 'no'; anything beyond this comes from the evil one." What falls into "beyond this"? Guilt for your answer, yep. Judgment because of your answer, yes. The demand for an explanation, yep. Jesus is all about simplicity and grace. He wants us to be honest about where we are at and have the freedom to honor it.

Jesus did a lot of healing, feeding, teaching, and caring for others during His short time on Earth. I remember being told that people were never angry at Him for healing the sick or feeding the hungry, but people did get mad at Him for the things He said. In a small way, I think life can be the same for us. There are people around us who are willing to be near when we can do something for them, but when we are tapped out or decide to create boundaries, there is an immediate shift in attitude.

As we follow Jesus through Matthew, we see Him heal a man with leprosy, speak with a centurion, calm a storm, raise a girl from the dead, teach parables, feed five thousand, and walk on water. During this time, Jesus is being followed around by the Pharisees, who are constantly trying to accuse Him of unlawfulness; despite Jesus's miracles and teachings, cities still won't repent, and John the Baptist is beheaded. In all of this, the word *withdrew* comes up three times. Withdrawing is an action or state of being where someone steps back, retires, or retreats. I picture Jesus with a heavy heart, saddened by people's lack of faith, injustice, and religious leaders' violent hatred. I imagine Him potentially overwhelmed and in need of some serious R and R. Proverbs 17:22 says, "A joyful heart is good medicine, but a crushed spirit dries up the bones." Have you ever heard the saying, "You can't fill up others' cups before your own"? I believe this is a picture of that saying. We need our time with our Father for comfort, understanding, and rest. If we invest in ourselves and our relationship with our Savior, we are best equipped to invest in others.

We also associate boundary setting with saying "no," and "no" feels like a bad word. As a recovering people pleaser, I have discovered that I can use this word respectfully, kindly, and freely. Conversely, "yes" is also a part of boundary setting. Know when to use both words. I greatly recommend Lysa Terkhurst's *The Best Yes* to dig deeper into the power of yes and no and how to confidently know when you want to use them. And while I am here recommending reading, I highly suggest *The Power of Vulnerability*, by Brené Brown, in which she discusses vulnerability being an act of courage rather than weakness. One of her stories talks about a spinning ring she purchased on her fortieth birthday.

When a request is made of her, she spins the ring three times while repeating the motto "Choose discomfort over resentment." Not fulfilling a need for someone may be a tough choice and complex answer to give, but so is dealing with the bitterness that comes from placing yourself last. Most people won't recognize when you aren't honoring your time or goals because a schedule gets busier and busier with invitations, demands, and petitions. That's where honesty with ourselves and with people in our lives come into the picture. Rachel Hollis's book *Girl, Wash Your Face* (another great read!) talks about how we value the commitments we make to others and how we disregard the promises we have made to ourselves. People don't know if you don't tell them, and most of the time, in your honesty, you'll be met with encouragement and support. On the rare occasion you aren't met with respect when putting yourself first, remember it's a discipline, and commitment is sometimes difficult. Stick to your guns because boundaries are both necessities and gifts. Resilience is like a muscle, developed over time and with consistency. The hard part about boundaries is setting them. The good part is that they can change when you do.

Here are a few boundaries I put into practice that have helped me:

> **1. I spend more time with God.** Read your Bible. Pray. A foundation rooted in God promotes so much healing and understanding.
>
> **2. I got off Facebook.** Facebook is an environment where I can easily get sucked into comparing my life with others. Conversely, this is also a place I can unknowingly create comparison issues for someone else, regardless of my intentions. If I do it, I'm betting others fall into the same crappy trap, and I don't want to perpetuate it.
>
> **3. I have intentionally developed the habit of being surrounded by people, media, and conversation that inspires me, encourages me, and challenges me to grow.**

- What is your initial impression of boundary setting? Does it make you uncomfortable?

- Does it feel rude or selfish?

- Start small. What do you need just for today?

- How can you be true to yourself?

- How can boundary setting help you while you deal with infertility?

Where'd That Come From?

A month ago, Caden, the son of my twin sister, Lauren, turned one. Without being too specific about Lauren's private medical history, I will share she, too, struggled with miscarriages and infertility before having Caden. Each pregnancy, fear of miscarriage stole the place where excitement and dreaming should have been. As Caden's pregnancy progressed, family and friends eagerly anticipated his arrival. I can honestly say during Lauren's pregnancy, I didn't contend with too much jealousy, and there were a couple of reasons why. First, because she experienced the heartbreak of infertility too. Most of the time, my focus was on the relief I felt, knowing one of us would have children. Having both gone through the worry and fear of infertility, our relationship took on an ally-type feel. There were certainly moments of envy—I'm not infallible—however, they were not memorable enough to go into detail on.

The second and most important reason jealousy wasn't an issue was God-given wisdom. He gave me the forethought to seek Him from the very beginning. Looking back on those nine months, I am incredibly grateful I was proactive in my relationship with Christ. I knew I wouldn't be able to rely on my flimsy abilities and habits. It's the same idea as staying ahead of pain by taking prescribed medication after a complicated surgery and a long recovery rather than allowing the unbearable pain to overwhelm you. I was fully aware that watching Lauren experience pregnancy would be a daily reminder of the opportunity I would not have. I dove into reading Scripture, I prayed wherever and whenever I needed to, and I thankfully fell into a habit of a lot of quiet time to be able to process how I was feeling. I found ultimate comfort, indescribable peace, and sweet joy that flourished, overpowering any jealousy that did sprout up.

I'm praying the truth in this chapter motivates you, if you're in a time where a friend or sibling is pregnant, to pursue God in a fuller, more active way than ever before. Second Corinthians 1:3–4 says, "Blessed be the God and Father of our Lord Jesus Christ, the Father of mercies and God of all comfort, who comforts us in our affliction, so that we may be able to comfort those who are in any affliction, with the comfort with which we ourselves are comforted by God."

I have learned how I respond to grief, how elemental a support system is, and how grace and shame can exist in a person all at the same time. Out of those lessons comes this book, with the intention to help you work through your grief, support your journey, and prove to you that grace trumps shame any day.

Lauren invited me into the birthing room with full disclosure that she would understand if I didn't accept. Lauren had severe preeclampsia in her third trimester, leaving no part of her left unswollen or uncomfortable, making it pretty clear that Caden would arrive before his due date. Twenty-seven days early, on February 1, the little man came after nine minutes of pushing. Watching her give birth was unlike any experience I have ever had! Time stopped, I considered changing my profession to labor and delivery nurse, and I cried uncontrollably from the beautiful intensity of the moment. I left the birthing room immediately after Caden's delivery so the new parents could have time to absorb the reality that they were now a family of three. I left the maternity floor in search of cold air and a place to pace. All the fear, excitement, nerves, and love had created an intense adrenaline rush!

Outside the hospital, I found relief, both physically and mentally, with a hearty cry session and chilly air. I was powerfully moved by God's creation of a new life and how He designed its start. I was grateful beyond words Caden was here, at last, safe and healthy beside his mama. As I continued to cry, my thoughts moved on to how Mike and I wouldn't have the same experience. We will never announce excitedly to our families, we will never feel the first kick, we will never be celebrated at a baby shower, and we will never be in a delivery room together, lovingly bringing a life into the world. This was one of those pockets of time when processing those thoughts started instantaneously. On a sidewalk, underneath the windows where my newest nephew was cuddling with his mom, I was grieving what would not happen for us. As I write this, I understand the "nevers" just mean we will have a different adventure, and that creates a fresh hope, but the mixture of love and heartache felt like it could've cracked me in two on the sidewalk that afternoon.

Throughout Caden's first year, I started seeing a counselor to focus on infertility's emotional toll on me. My appointments became an opportunity to thoroughly examine an experience or emotion without fear of judgment. We discussed practical ways to recognize, evaluate, and accept my current limitations. In the sessions, I became more comfortable sharing what was on my mind and how I was feeling and began to determine where boundaries needed to be established to maintain self-care. For some people, including myself, counseling holds a stigma. My initial perception of counseling was an hour-long appointment where I would talk, and the counselor would dole out righteous advice I obviously missed.

In my sessions, my therapist and I have a discussion, narrowing down essential details about an event and coming to a conclusion on how to best approach handling the situation. At length, my counselor and I have discussed the circumstances of Mike and me, and she was the first person to help me understand the depression I was dealing with was because I was grieving. One moment you can feel like you have completely moved past what you're dealing with, and the next moment, it can be as raw and abrupt as if you were just diagnosed again. I encourage you: if you haven't sought out this avenue of care, please do.

Let's fast-forward to Caden's first birthday party. The family was in town to celebrate, the cutest dinosaurs were ready to be placed out for decoration, and the day had very little stress. At the head of the room, Caden was ceremoniously placed in his high chair to eat his cake. Family and friends immediately surrounded his seat, blocking the view from where my aunt and I were sitting. I quickly became infuriated at other people's rudeness and their general lack of thought when it came to anyone else. My mind was bitter…mean thought after bitter, mean thought. The one thing I have come to realize about myself is that I use anger to avoid being sad. Identifying this tactic isn't something I'm good at calling out in the heat of the moment. All of a sudden, a lump formed in my throat, and my eyes began to water. I got up, turned around, and tried to drink all the water I had in my cup to relieve the mounting pressure. This lump was not going away, and I knew I would not be able to stop this sudden need to cry. Without a word to anyone, I grabbed my coat, walked out to my car, sat in the back seat, and began to sob. I don't think I got a second into it before Mike knocked on the window to see why I left. He climbed into the back and held me until I was finished. See why I named the chapter the way I have?

As time has passed since our diagnosis, I feel like I have accepted our reality and even enjoyed the freedom our circumstance has created. I have had fewer episodes of anger, jealousy, and denial, and have worked diligently to address my depression. I was feeling strong! Proud! Untouchable! Where'd that come from?

My mom said it best the other day: "Sometimes the scab heals a little, only to be picked right off again." She was referring to my being told by another friend about her current pregnancy. I go from watching one pregnancy to another, to another. I know my friend was nervous to tell me, not because she thought I'd react badly but because she knew that her news, although wonderful, would rekindle my sadness at our childlessness. In those times, I feel like a Dementor from the Harry Potter series. They were soulless creatures who gradually deprived people of their happiness just by being in their presence. I expected life to have trials like grieving death or financial bumps, but I never imagined being the antagonist of my own story.

The enemy had done it again. I'd become susceptible to a lie through a half-truth. I am strong, but just because I was overcome with emotion as Caden smeared first-birthday smash cake everywhere, it didn't make me weak, and it didn't mean I was back to square one. One of my biggest fears is falling back into the dissatisfied and exhausted girl I had become immediately after our diagnosis. Nevertheless, despite the progress I have made, it doesn't guarantee I won't have a setback or two. Exploring and acknowledging my grief doesn't mean that I have conquered jealousy, sadness, or anger.

A situation like this is where my head's knowledge about extending grace and my heart's choice to accept it are in harmony. In other words, this is where the rubber meets the road for me: Do I believe what I say? Will I allow myself to embrace grace? The truth is, it is much easier for me to extend grace and preach grace than to allow myself to enter its reality. Throughout our journey, grace has become more than just a word. The sweetness of grace is at those banquet tables I described earlier on; it is the gift God gives when I know I need it. Grace is in the choices I make to give myself time to reconcile my emotions. My "me time" is when I crawl into bed; cuddle my dog, Wrigley; and binge-watch *The Golden Girls*.

What are your beliefs about grace? Why do we make receiving grace so difficult? Maybe this time in your life feels like grace is far away. Do you feel undeserving? Or perhaps you've just never really explored what grace has to offer.

Grace is everywhere in the Bible, both explicitly and obscurely. Here are a few of my favorite direct verses about grace:

- Romans 11:6 says, "But if it is by grace, it is no longer based on works; otherwise grace would no longer be grace."

- You can't earn it, nor should you feel the need. We are working on enough in this lifetime through temptation and sin, which is why grace was established. It is an extension of God's character and love for us.

- Hebrews 4:16 says, "Let us then with confidence draw near to the throne of grace, that we may receive mercy and find grace to help in time of need."

- I love how the author of Hebrews describes going to the throne of grace confidently. Confidence is built on practice. Sometimes the most straightforward option is the hardest. As humans, we definitely can overcomplicate things.

- John 1:16 says, "And from his fullness, we have all received, grace upon grace."

- This gift is aboundingly free because Jesus is, was, and will always be. He came here, lived a sin-free life, died for my sin, and rose three days later. When God looks at me, He sees Jesus first, and He is what makes me whole.

Grace can be found as a subtly woven thread throughout biblical stories too. Elijah the prophet is a guy I feel like I can relate to. He had significant highs and significant lows in his faith journey, and as a believer grappling with the whys'" and "how comes" of infertility, I have my own faith crossroads. In 1 Kings 16:29–34, we find that Ahab has become king of Israel, married Jezebel, and started serving and worshipping Baal. Baal was believed to produce crops, grant fertility, and control the sun and storms. The Bible records that Ahab "aroused the anger of the Lord, the God of Israel, [more] than did all the kings of Israel before him" (1 Kings 16:33). Ahab had one of the worst track records where God was concerned, and to make matters worse, he had misled God's people, and the worship of Baal had now become widespread among Israel.

In chapter 17, God sends Elijah to tell Ahab, "There will be no rain in the next few years except at my word" (v. 1). God's choice in consequences is a direct hit at what the people believe Baal can provide. I think this is our first glimpse of grace. Despite their wrongful worship, God was faithful in meeting the needs of the people of Israel. I imagine that when Ahab received this warning, he had very little concern. God was responsible for the country's continued care, and Ahab grew dependent and secure while giving credit to a god that didn't exist. Elijah's prophecy comes to settle on the land and pressure mounts on Ahab. His solution is to hunt Elijah down without success.

Three years later, Elijah, who had been in hiding and cared for by God, was directed to return. He tells Ahab, "Now summon the people from all over Israel to meet me on Mount Carmel. And bring the four hundred and fifty prophets of Baal and the four hundred prophets of Asherah (according to their belief this was Baal's sister, a fertility goddess associated with the stars) who eat at Jezebel's table" (1 Kings 18:19). Soon we find a crowd has gathered on the mount, and two altars have been set up: one for Elijah and one for believers of Baal. The terms: "Get two bulls for us. Let Baal's prophets choose one for themselves, and let them cut it into pieces and put it on the wood but not set fire to it. I will prepare the other bull and put it on the wood but not set fire to it. Then you call on the name of your god, and I will call on the name of the Lord. The God who answers by fire—he is God" (1 Kings 18:23, 24). Elijah even soaks the bull, wood, and land around his offering. Soon "the fire of the Lord fell and burned up the sacrifice, the wood, the stones, and the soil and also licked up the water in the trench" (1 Kings 18:38). What a major spiritual victory! If I had been Elijah, I'd like to think I'd be fist-pumping the air and reveling in all of God's glory!

Instead, we find our leading man on the run! What happened? Jezebel "sent a messenger to Elijah to say, 'May the gods deal with me, be it ever so severely if by this time tomorrow I do not make your life like that of one of them'" (1 Kings 19:2). Jezebel is threatening to kill him, and he runs. We find him by himself in the wilderness, praying to die:

> "I have had enough, Lord," he said. "Take my life; I am no better than my ancestors." Then he lay down under the bush and fell asleep. All at once, an angel touched him and said, "Get up and eat." He looked around, and there by his head was some bread baked over hot coals and a jar of water. He ate and drank and then lay down again. The angel of the Lord came back a second time and touched him and said, "Get up and eat, for the journey is too much for you." So he got up and ate and drank. Strengthened by that food, he traveled forty days and forty nights until he reached Horeb, the mountain of God. (1 Kings 19:4–8 NIV)

God did not abandon Elijah. God did not get frustrated or angry by Elijah's emotional regression. God fed him. It allowed him to work through that fear and intense discouragement. God acknowledged that at that moment, "the journey [was] too much for [him]" (1 Kings 19:7) and advocated rest. The word grace isn't seen once in this passage, but it covers Elijah. Elijah doesn't deny God's care or argue that he shouldn't have it or doesn't want it. He accepts this grace gratefully. He eats his food, and he rests. The concept may seem absurd that Elijah "allowed" God to care for him, but from my viewpoint, we either draw near to God, or we draw away from God.

Please don't misunderstand; I'm not placing judgment, but our relationship with Christ isn't designed to be stagnant. We're either growing or withering; there is no middle ground. Both choices have their hardships. I have been in the place of questioning and placing blame on God. I have been brought now to a place of grieving with God and seeking His comfort. As I sit and think about the harmful habits I was using after our diagnosis to "cope" to my current practices, God has led me to like rest and open communication with Mike. I acknowledge that using those tools is a practiced discipline. Asking for help and receiving help doesn't come easily to me, but my loving, gentle Father is ready to do that.

Elijah had big highs and some lows, and the same with me and my emotions. We don't have to have it all figured out. We just have to allow God to go through it with us. Sometimes you will have good days, periods where you're impervious to your infertility, and then there will be moments where you'll be surprised by what interrupted your emotional winning streak. The point is, it happens, and preparation may not be an option. If and when you find yourself in a "Where'd that come from?" moment, give yourself the grace you deserve to acknowledge your feelings, work your way through it, and find rest when you need it. And remember, always look for Jesus. He is the protagonist in every story: Elijah's, mine, and yours.

Mike and I held each other in the car for about ten minutes. We cleaned up and went back to the party. Later, we talked at home, I cried some more, and we lay down, holding each other, and watched *The Golden Girls*.

- What does giving yourself grace look like?

- What verse or story resonates with you when reading about grace?

- Have you been discouraged by sudden emotion?

Marriage

Matthew 19:5 says, "For this reason a man will leave his father and mother and be united to his wife, and the two shall become one flesh."

"One flesh" conjures up a variety of strange, distorted images. As if you just popped into *The Matrix* movie. We aren't actually morphed into a collective body; however, just like our individual selves can't be divided into pieces and still be whole, neither can we look at our lives the same after marriage. Yes, I am a fully functioning, independent person even though I am married, but my choices and actions no longer affect only me. God's design for marriage takes two ordinary individuals and forms one extraordinary creation. The phrase "one flesh" is both a descriptive analogy and a direct reality, albeit a mysterious one.

I remember when Mike and I were dating, people would tell us marriage would change our relationship. I'd roll my eyes in the what-do-you-know fashion and go on about my day. Other than starting my eagerly anticipated sex life, what more could change? When I got married,

I understood what they meant, although it was hard to describe, and in all honesty, it still is after eight years. I feel inextricably connected to Mike. We make decisions together and plan days, weeks, and months around our individual schedules; at the end of each day, we prepare a meal to enjoy, talk, and then fall asleep holding each other. If I no longer had Mike, it would feel as if a limb were missing. I would have to learn to cope with how to function while fully aware I'm not complete anymore. The physical, emotional, and spiritual effect this relationship has on me proves I need to make it a top priority.

When I think about the hierarchy of my relationships, I tend to envision a food-pyramid-like structure. The foundation starts with God. His piece of the pyramid is the widest part of the triangle, supporting all the other subsequent sections. When my relationship with God is in order, all my other relationships benefit. The quality of my relationship with Him is crucial to the stability of the different levels. My intentional investment in God is also an investment in my marriage, family, and friends. The more time I spend with Jesus, the more influence He has developing compassion for His people, showing me where my faults lie in situations, and how I can mature in my responses. I have learned a lot about myself through Christ's eyes, and only with Christ can I overcome, change, and evolve in a positive direction.

The second level is my marriage. Naturally, we bring a host of individual issues along with us into our marriage: trauma, expectations, insecurities, self-absorption, difficult childhoods, past relationships, gender role definition, divorce...Mike and I have known each other for sixteen years and have been married for eight. We will forever be working on ourselves as individuals and our union as a whole. We will never have it completely figured out, despite our progress through communication, quality time, counseling, and support. No marriage is flawless. It requires effort and protection to safeguard us from what the enemy throws at us in a lifetime.

Continue to learn about each other, deepen your friendship, explore your intimate life, and be the example of love to your spouse that you want to receive. Note I didn't say, "Be *an* example." I said, "Be *the* example." You're setting a precedent, inspiring your spouse to behave or act similarly. I choose to be conscientious about my attitude and what kind of vibes I am giving off at home. Am I pessimistic? Am I more concerned with what he is doing, how he is doing it, and why? Or am I engaging with him? Intentionally doing things around the house that will benefit both of us?

Please hear me, I am not asking you to be a bubbly, bouncy whirlwind of energy and joy or a slave. Some days you're going to have a hard day, maybe from work or interaction with the family that can be a real mood killer, but invite your spouse into what happened, how you're feeling, and what you need. Please don't make it a passive-aggressive mystery. Give them a chance to understand and perhaps change your attitude. The other pieces I have to keep a close eye on and constantly evaluate are my expectations. Are they fair? How were they developed, and does he hold the same belief? Do I hold myself to be equal to the standard

I require? The biggest expectation I've had to let go of is he can't read my mind.

Realistically, I have known he does not have this power, and being honest, I am grateful this is not an option, but culturally there is a long-held belief or argument that men should just "know." The first few years I was married, I had a hard time understanding how he couldn't see what needed to be done around the house or what bills had come in and needed payment or that relaxing for me is an impossibility if there is a to-do list in my head. Key phrase: *In my head*. I had inadvertently created the guideline I would manage all these things because I took the responsibilities over, never speaking about a division of chores I needed when overwhelmed with them. I didn't trust him to do (insert chore here) as well as I would. *Big* mistake. This setup wasn't going to work for our marriage, and understanding this was invaluable and incredibly impactful! Long lesson shortened: If I need it, I have to verbalize it.

Marriage itself is an earthly parable, an illustration of Christ and the Church. A purposeful design and a deliberate parallel. God ordained a permanent union between His Son and the Church, and marriage is our earthly reflection. Acknowledging how critical it is not to overlook this detail restores the context of marriage regarding our priorities. Christ demonstrates how we should act in marriage: selfless, patient, caring, merciful, faithful, obedient, and loving. Most of these attributes do not come naturally or easily to me. Marrying Mike has been the most challenging, most rewarding, most intense, and most remarkably significant choice I have ever made. One of the aspects of our marriage I am infinitely grateful to be blessed with is that I don't have to be worried about my needs because I know that Mike worries about them for me. He models Ephesians 5:25 willfully, and his actions call me to a higher standard.

The next layer on the pyramid would be children. Whether we are given a chance to be parents or an aunt and uncle or mentor, the focus we set on our marriage now will be an advantage to any children God places in our lives, now or later. When Mike and I were in premarital counseling, he was fiercely adamant about sleeping in the same room without exception. Making the statement not to sleep in the same room when you're angry feels like a weapon that would only create a further divide. Throwing kids into the mix who may see that could create feelings of instability, adding a compromised home atmosphere. I've truly loved this policy! I still feel excited when I get to sleep next to him every night. Bedtime feels like the ultimate sleepover with my best friend, plus benefits! The point is, however we take care of our marriage now, kids will see its fruit, whether ripe or rotten.

Topping off the pyramid are the last two levels: family/friends and acquaintances. Each relationship has its own compartment with lines purposely distinguishing boundaries. The friends' level can't influence the marriage level, and the kids' level doesn't come before God. Each section creates a whole triangle centered around fulfillment, order, and happiness. This concept has been easy for me to grasp mentally but hard to put into practice.

As friends have made plans to conceive and have been successful within months of discussing starting a family, Mike and I stopped at first base. We have decided to approach this season with open minds, appreciating the freedom that not having kids creates. I have been told numerous times how "lucky" we are not to have kids and how we should joyously embrace our independence. Each time infuriated me because of how callous the advice was, but I found they had a point once I got past the initial sting. I am not saying infertility is a privilege or that I jump for joy at my diagnosis; however, I needed to be flexible to welcome joy back for my own sake. Yes, I want my life to be filled with baby snuggles, horribly funny diapers-gone-wrong stories, and the excitement of first steps. The fact of the matter is, it's up to us to remain present in our reality and focus on appreciating it. Mike reminds me of this continuously as we take our time Saturday mornings, leisurely getting out of bed, on impromptu trips to the botanical gardens, and on wine-and-cheese date nights. Babies don't stop people from living, but they do change the way they now manage life. Our circumstances have made it, so our life continues the way it is.

Since our diagnosis, I have deliberately been more observant about our blessings versus what we don't have. This thought process is a definite paradigm shift that took years to cultivate for me. Even after establishing the discipline of positivity during infertility, I have been made to feel as if my attitude is a symptom of a subconscious desire not to be a parent, and I should be more oppressed emotionally by our situation. Other times society has made me feel like, "Why aren't you over it?" Bizarre, right? I understand that my emotional well-being will never make everyone happy, and my reactions will either be not enough or too much for people.

In marriage, we can get complacent in our relationship, using commitment as an excuse to stop pursuing one another, especially when going through difficult times. The dedication to not lose sight of why we chose to spend our lives together is imperative. Mike and I have grieved our circumstances differently as individuals. Still, we have chosen to be open with each other in our grief, which has been foundational in being a united front. When I close off from Mike, I place our relationship on the back burner and then forget to nurture it.

One method Mike and I use to reassure one another is looking for a way to satisfy the other person's love language, while also being aware of their expressions of love. A love language is how we show and experience love. The five are:

1. Quality time

2. Physical touch

3. Words of affirmation

4. Gift giving or receiving

5. Acts of service

Mike and I discovered how we express love is different than how we receive it. Receiving words of affirmation from Mike is how I feel loved. An unexpected card or text checking in on me throughout the day makes me feel thought about and special. Gift giving is how I show Mike I love him. The excitement of going out and purchasing a game he's mentioned or surprising him with tickets to a concert he'd like to attend brings me joy. Physical touch is Mike's primary love language. Any intimacy—holding hands on a walk, hugging when we come home at night to each other, or making love—meets Mike's needs to feel he is loved. How he expresses his love is through acts of service. Mike is a hardworking, thoughtful man who goes out of his way to make my life simpler. Just yesterday, we rushed around completing necessary errands, only to feel slightly frustrated and exhausted when we got home. We had two loads of laundry to fold, and Mike insisted I jump in the shower to relax and unwind while he managed the chores.

The categories aren't hard-and-fast rules, but we understand that these are our core interactions. We are deliberate about meeting those needs for each other while also aiming to see how the other is naturally conveying love. Mike may not get me a card for a while, but he runs out last minute anytime I'm in the mood for a sweet. I struggle with initiating sex because I allow self-doubt to get the better of me; however, I'll always be Mike's wing girl at a comic convention. For further explanation and understanding, check out Gary Chapman's book *The Five*

Love Languages to better grasp the concepts because they are genuinely invaluable pieces of knowledge.

Jumping to one of the best parts I love about marriage…drumroll, please! Let's talk about…sex, baby. That's right; I went there. I threw in a lil salt and peppa. For real, though, God designed intimacy to express love in marriage, as a time to comfort one another, and for a mental and physical release from daily life.

Infertility is a laundry list of peeing on sticks, when to have sex and when not to, this test or that test, cycle days, and periods. It can be a real buzz kill on the sex life. Soon making love turns into a business transaction on the calendar. I remember feeling stressed and pressured when it was deemed the time we had to "do it." I despise calling lovemaking "doing it," but our intimacy had become an informal formality. When we got married, Mike and I were virgins, and I felt robbed of having this incredible, amazingly fun, and special connection, tainted by infertility.

Worry and fear of "Will we get pregnant this time?" and questions like "Did I not lie in bed long enough?" followed. Spontaneity became a thing of the past, and I missed it. Please don't get me wrong; I love being close with my husband, but books aren't wrong when they say men and women are built differently. Sex starts with my mood; if my needs are being met outside the bedroom (e.g., quality time, shared responsibilities, and spiritual leadership), adding the anxiety I was feeling about our infertility, getting in the mood was tough for me. My mental state was no reflection on Mike; it was just that my mind was so heavy with all the questions: Will it happen? Won't it happen? Should we be in this position or that position? How long should I lie after that? Is conception dependent on my orgasm because what happens if I didn't? Again, no reflection on Mike, but my mind is a powerful distraction. I hated even the pressure of worrying if my mind was going to let me enjoy the experience. If it isn't already clear, my mind works overtime on overthinking. Thanks, brain. In any case, I was relieved when the pressure of conception was over.

I wouldn't say being married for eight years is a long time; however, it is just enough time to establish routines, habits, and ruts. Add infertility appointments, timed intercourse, and intense mental and emotional worry; it can strain a marriage. We had to be deliberate about setting up date nights and overnight trips to our favorite hotel. Quality time spent at home investing in each other's interests has been a terrific habit we've created. What I am trying to get across is: Don't lose each other. Don't stop pursuing each other. Don't let infertility ruin your marriage. My hope for you after reading this chapter is that you take a long look at your marriage. Reclaim it! Infertility may stop me from having biological kids, but it cannot have my marriage.

- What were your hopes for your marriage before getting married?

- What does your marriage look like now? How can you improve on it?

- How can you show Christ to your spouse?

- Are you using the examples you saw as a kid to define who you are as a spouse or who you want to be as a parent? Is that the example you want to set?

- Is there a conversation that needs to happen about expectations?

- With what love language do you receive love? What one do you use to express love? How about your spouse?

Friendships

This book initially started as a journal, expressing to God how I felt, pouring out my grief and anger on paper. Slowly, God began to shift my perspective from what I was feeling two ways I could heal. He gave me ample time to accept our infertility. I found support through His word and the community of people Mike and I had and, when my heart was ready, counsel in areas of my life in need of renovation, like learning to rest and setting appropriate boundaries. I haven't necessarily gotten answers I thought I needed, like "What paths do Mike and I take now?" or "Why us?" But I have seen a glimpse of His purpose as I write about our experience. He has been gently exchanging my dream for His dream for me. I am applying what God is teaching me in my journey through infertility and in every aspect of my life, which brings me to the topic of friendships.

God created us in His image, which instilled in us a deep relational desire. Our God is triune: three in one, the Father, the Son, and the Spirit. The three are constantly interacting, never separate but wholly distinct. He created animals in pairs and expressed concern and quick action for Adam's loneliness by finishing creation with Eve. We as humans enjoy company, crave community, and often covet relationships others have.

I have come back to this chapter repeatedly because friendships have been one of the toughest casualties of my infertility experience. The topic is challenging because evaluating my friendships makes me aware of the responsibilities that lie with me when establishing a relationship. God is showing me what true friendship looks like, how it's developed and maintained, and what unhealthy friendships I have invested in. I didn't expect this journey to be fertile ground for examining this area in my life. Ultimately, my goal is to create friendships that matter and have a purpose for both people involved. I have clear intentions to develop a community around me that challenges me, supports me, invests in me, and shows authentic compassion. Proverbs 27:17 says, "As iron sharpens iron, so one man sharpens another," reminding me that ultimately the people we let into our lives have the potential to influence our attitudes and character, and we them.

Some people may read this and argue I am exclusive and that we should be friends with everyone; however, God designed relationships to hold a purpose, making that belief system unfounded. One of the things I learned this year is the theological term *imago Dei*, which is a phrase that expresses the connection between God and His creation. Genesis 1:27 tells us "God created man in his own image…" The passage doesn't mean that God is a human, but that we take after God's likeness in our moral, spiritual, and intellectual nature. *Imago Dei* is the action of recognizing and participating in loving God and loving others as an expression of God. We don't have to be friends with everyone, but we have to respect them as people with stories and feelings.

In Luke 22:28 Jesus tells the disciples, "You are those who stood by me in my trials." Jesus specifically chose the twelve disciples as friends He could share his heart with, glorifying God in each relationship. Jesus loved everyone He came across while He lived but was deliberately intimate with His disciples.

I had always wanted that best friend experience. The Kimmy to my D. J., the Carlton to my Will, or better yet my own Golden Girls' posse…I think you may get the picture, and if not, please google the '90s (the best decade ever). In my search for that, I discovered two things: (1) I am lucky enough to have those relationships in my family with my parents, sisters, and husband, and (2) I need to be more discerning about who I am friends with, where I am accountable in repairing friendships, and being open to new ones.

Trust is essential when developing a relationship; trust with what you share and knowing they have your best interest at heart. Genuine friends are present in their interaction with you, respect your feelings, value accountability, are willing to forgive, are dependable, and are ready to come around you in hard times.

Esther is one of my all-time favorite books in the Bible, considering she's one fierce lady and because God isn't mentioned outright in the book. The significance of God not being directly referenced exemplifies how God works behind the scenes. The book of Esther details no miracles or outright intervention, but instead focuses on God's redemption through the critical situational placement of Esther's queenship and familial relation to Mordecai. Mordecai quickly becomes a thorn in Haman's side, a distinguished noble in King Xerxes's circle, when he chooses not to kneel and pay honor to Haman.

A few ideas behind Mordecai's defiance are that he didn't bow down because the action could potentially express idolatry which went against his religious principle. Another more historical reason is the tension that developed early on between Amalek and the Jews. Haman is mentioned as an Agagite, a relation linked to the Amalekites. Mordecai, a descendant of Saul and the tribe of Benjamin, would likely recall the war between the two groups during Israel's exodus. Emboldened by suspicion, jealousy, fear, and entitlement of the land (not a good combination), the Amalekites went to war to stop the Israelites' progress. Esther chapter 3:2 records "all the royal officials at the king's gate knelt down and paid honor to Haman… [but Mordecai]." Verses 5 and 6 tell us, "When Haman saw that [he] would not kneel down or pay him the honor, he was enraged. Yet having learned who Mordecai's people were, he scorned the idea of killing only Mordecai. Instead, Haman looked for a way to destroy all Mordecai's people, the Jews, throughout the whole kingdom of Xerxes."

Can't control your temper? Haman's character is on intense display. We can quickly infer he's reckless, immature, spiteful, and greedy. So why is he important to our friendship chapter? Because he was friends with King Xerxes, Esther's husband. Haman takes it upon himself to take advantage of his position and relationship to manipulate the king:

> Then Haman said to King Xerxes, "There is a certain people dispersed among the peoples in all the provinces of your kingdom who keep themselves separate. Their customs are different from those of all other people, and they do not obey the king's laws; it is not in the king's best interest to tolerate them. If it pleases the king, let a decree be issued to destroy them, and I will give ten thousand talents of silver to the king's administrators for the royal treasury." (Esther 3:8–9, NIV)

Haman is a selfish, violent man, which isn't a good attribute in a friend at all. However, Xerxes has his responsibility in the matter. Let's see how he responds: "So the king took his signet ring from his finger and gave it to Haman, son of Hammedatha, the Agagite, the enemy of the Jews" (Esther 3:10).

Xerxes doesn't investigate Haman's claims, doesn't question his motives, and doesn't know his character well enough before putting him in a position of power. Here's the one other miscalculation on Haman's part: Esther is a Jew. By blatantly trusting Haman, Xerxes is flippantly willing to approve genocide and haphazardly places his wife, whom "[he] was attracted to more than any other women, and [who] won his favor and approval" (2:17) in mortal danger.

Generally speaking, most of us don't experience extreme Hamanlike people or relationships, but I know we often continue to participate in one-sided friendships. Friendships with agendas where their needs are met with no concern for yours. For my own sanity, I have to believe the people who adopt the practice of exploiting relationships to their advantage are not consciously aware they're doing it. Conversely, their lack of awareness of their self-centeredness places them at a disadvantage of being aware of others.

When Mike and I officially decided to begin trying to have children, I had a friend out of state who decided to try at the same time. We had developed a friendship through personal dream-filled letters, and I believed our relationship had great potential. We had shared our goals and told each other funny stories; I had gone to her during a difficult season in my marriage and dreamed about being neighbors with our families growing side by side. Each month we would lament over the phone about not getting pregnant and worry about why. The conversations would end with words of encouragement, advice to relax, and talk about being neighbors in chaotic harmony.

Three months in, when she conceived, I was incredibly happy for her! She took weekly progress photos, and I felt both excited and hopeful that Mike and I wouldn't be far behind. Mike and I received our diagnosis during her pregnancy, which I chose not to share with her because I didn't want to steal any of her happiness. In other words, I didn't want to be the Harry Potter Dementor I'd felt like I had become when others shared their pregnancy announcements. When her baby was born, I booked a flight out to visit and meet him. At that visit, I shared with her that Mike and I couldn't have children, and her response both hurt and shocked me. She said, "Well, I guess it wasn't meant to be." It was going to be a long three days. The visit got even more awkward while we watched episode after episode of *16 and Pregnant* and a Netflix documentary on infertile couples who decided to adopt monkeys as their children. I kid you not. Do I think her TV choices were intentional? No. Should I have said something? Yes. Her choices in what we watched felt like a blatant disregard for my feelings, and her lack of sensitivity stunned me.

Here was a person I was investing in who couldn't see past herself even to take a glimpse at how much I was hurting. I frequently wonder if situations were reversed, how others would feel and how I would respond. That thought process has cultivated my aim in listening purposefully and attempting to place myself in other people's positions. Eventually, she moved back to our home state, and we run into each other now and again, but we haven't rebuilt any connection. Effort is a two-way street and a requirement of a foundational relationship. Her response and interaction during my visit were paramount in discovering how unbalanced our friendship was. It has been two years since any real personal interaction, and when I look back, I can see my desire for a best friend influenced my glorification of the friendship I built in my head versus what was truly there. And in fairness I was not in a place to understand or know how to support her as a new mom. This relationship taught me that people could be in your life for a season to serve a purpose; you can be thankful for the experience and accept the end as the only closure you need.

Naturally, there will be times friends answer unsympathetically, and advice will be given without experience or knowledge of what going through infertility is like. It will be up to you how you manage those times—perhaps being more honest about what you're experiencing and the feelings that come with it or setting boundaries on safe or unsafe topics. The other day I was with a beautiful friend who got on the subject of all the pregnant women at church, beginning to name them off happily, and I stopped her midname because I knew the conversation would have no positive effect for me. I know her intention was not to hurt me, and in most social settings, having this conversation wouldn't matter, but for me and my heart, it did, and it was my responsibility to share that with her.

The book of Proverbs is all about wisdom; a characteristic God places very highly as a pursuit of believers: "Blessed is the one who finds wisdom, and the one who gets understanding" (3:13). We are told wisdom is "more precious than rubies, and nothing [we] can desire compares with her" (8:11). Knowledge is often gained when you're open to receiving it. That means seeing experiences as a chance to learn, being self-aware enough to admit fault, accept the consequences, and discern when there needs to be restitution.

I was incredibly fortunate enough to work with Emily, a young lady I went to junior high with. We knew each other in school but didn't have the same friends, so we never really connected. The day I started my first job as a massage therapist was also her first day as an office manager at our chiropractic office. I walked in, nervous, a bundle of knots in my stomach, a laundry basket full of crisply folded sheets, and an eager desire to help people. The knots were winning out for my attention; however, upon noticing Emily, I was thankful to see a familiar young face. We became good friends over time. I grew to know her family, and she mine. We talked deeply about our personal stories and hugged each other when words were not enough, and I was quickly honored by her request to stand up at her wedding.

As with each story, Em became pregnant. She knew my history and was intentional about telling me privately and gently. We grew distant during her pregnancy. I felt left behind; I was dealing with jealousy again, which was getting old, and I worried that not having the convenience of seeing each other every day at work would drastically affect our friendship. Emily soon left the office for motherhood; she had significant transitions in her wake, life got busy, and I decided I didn't want to be the first one to reach out. Or "stubbornly refused to" may be a better way of putting it.

Thankfully, after a few months, she texted asking to get together but saying she understood if I didn't want to. I did want to, really badly. I missed her company, advice, and sense of humor, and hearing her crazy stories and wonderfully creative ideas. We got together and had an honest conversation about how we didn't know how to talk about what the other person was going through. Thankfully, Emily and I have reconnected, and I have been blessed to be reminded of the beauty she brings into my life. Proverbs 27:9 tells us, "Perfume and incense bring joy to the heart, and the pleasantness of one's friend springs from [her] earnest counsel."

I came to see that what stood between me and a friendship was a complicated conversation. I told her I had become jealous and hurt because I didn't feel acknowledged. She told me she worried about being a reminder to me and didn't know how to check in. I can't give a formula on how to have this conversation or what should be said, except being honest and open with each other. Whether you're dealing with a similar situation or maybe feeling unsupported, odds are you both don't know what to say to the other.

Jesus is our best example of how to be a friend, what to look for in a friendship, and how to respond admirably when faced with difficult situations within them. "Greater love has no man than this: that he lay down his life for his friends" (John 15:13), so said the greatest friend of all.

- Is there a friendship that has been affected by infertility?

- How can you do your part in repairing it?

- Is there a friendship that has made you feel it may be a seasonal experience because of infertility?

Advice

I moved out when I was twenty-one. My parents had advised me against moving out so soon after getting established in my job. They pointed out the opportunity I had to enjoy low-cost living while saving money without the stress of many responsibilities. I truly enjoyed my parents' company. My mom cooked delicious homemade meals; she was always up for braiding my hair and playing a cribbage game. Dad was readily available for a good laugh or in-depth conversation, and they both respected my privacy. In other words, life was good—really good. My sisters had both been moved out and married by twenty, making me feel like I was behind the curve. Oh, the joy that comes with comparing! Headstrong and feeling the need to flex my independence, I decided I knew better and moved out to the building next door.

When I reflect on my decisions, I often wish I had taken my parents' advice. I ended up not liking living alone and invited Mike to move in with me while we were dating, placing us in the position of sexual temptation. Anxiety and worry were frequent feelings as I learned the art of budgeting. Once, after paying all the bills, I was twenty dollars short of affording to do laundry. Two sleepless nights went by as I berated myself for my evident stupidity at my failure. Thoughts don't wash clothes, though, and that pile was increasing. The next day I told my mom in the car between crying jags of my many disappointments, while asking for the twenty dollars I needed, and she said, "Amber, it's twenty bucks and no big deal. You're doing great, and I'm proud of you. Let's stop crying and go do your laundry." My goodness, I love that woman.

Mike and I still managed to live independently, growing up together as we navigated the ups and downs of overseeing a household. I don't regret any of what we've lived through because those experiences ultimately brought me to the place I am today. However, some of what we came across and struggled with was unnecessary and avoidable, had I listened. Those first few years were undoubtedly humbling, knocking the I-know-better-than-you-do chip off my shoulder.

Since then, I have sought out advice in a hypervigilant way, as if I were polling people. My twenties have been a full-time project of taking survey after survey to collect opinions to find out how popular an option, idea, or piece of advice was. I take pride in being open-minded to different perspectives and respecting others' beliefs. I've always believed less talking and more listening helps me grow. The difference, I've learned, is listening is an action, relationally essential, and valuable to both parties. Still, when the conversation turns to the topic of my life, I have to be selective on the people I let speak. I also learned incessant polling is a red flag in an area where I don't have self-trust.

Early in our infertility story, the habit of wanting to know what others thought, what they might do in our circumstances, clogged my head and heart. Unhesitatingly, responses came in quick and effortless: "Take out a loan to have IVF" or "Fundraise for adoption because you don't want to go the route of foster care; those kids are damaged goods" or "Just enjoy life as free adults with no responsibilities; see how lucky you are" and "Just focus on being the best aunt and uncle you can be. You can borrow the kids, and when you've had enough, you can give them back to their parents." Some of the feedback hurt, and some of it was insensitive and uninformed, but I trust most of our friends and family were trying to be helpful about a situation that was as unfamiliar to them as it was to us.

According to Dictionary.com, advice is characterized as a response based on knowledge or experience. Opinions are beliefs or judgments that are formed without knowledge or experience. The answers we received fell into either the advice or opinion category, and sorting them out was like enduring a mad game of Bozo Buckets. Ninety-nine percent of the people I shared our story with had not gone through being told they could not have biological children, and over half of them didn't have to deal with an infertility diagnosis. The practice I developed after not accepting the wise guidance of my parents nine years ago created several problems for me:

1. I had to learn what constitutes an opinion or advice.

2. Major drawbacks like wasted time and decision paralysis came from too much advice.

3. I gained copious amounts of input ranging from decent to poor, requiring time and discipline in using my Bible to see if any of it held up to the wisdom found in Scripture.

Scripture emphasizes the importance of wisdom and the powerful characteristics that accompany its presence. Throughout Proverbs, you'll find verses like these:

> Blessed is the [woman] who finds wisdom, the [woman] who gains understanding, for she is more profitable than silver and yields better returns than gold. She is more precious than rubies; nothing you desire can compare with her. (3:13–15 NIV)

> Get wisdom, get understanding; do not forget my words or swerve from them. Do not forsake wisdom, and she will protect you; love her, and she will watch over you. Wisdom is supreme; therefore, get wisdom. Though it costs all you have, get understanding. Esteem her, and she will exalt you; embrace her, and she will honor you.

> She will set a garland of grace on your head
> and present you with a crown of splendor.
> (4:5–9 NIV)

Who wouldn't want their decision-making skills to be valued over treasured jewels or be known for their maturity through Christ? Sign me up! Proverbs also share essential instruction on how to establish a good foundation in the practice of being prudent:

- "A kindhearted woman gains respect, but ruthless men gain only wealth" (11:16 NIV).

- "A generous [woman] will prosper; [she] who refreshes others will [herself] be refreshed" (11:25 NIV).

- "An evil [woman] is trapped by [her] sinful talk, but a righteous [woman] escapes trouble" (12:13 NIV).

- "A gentle answer turns away wrath, but a harsh word stirs up anger" (15:1 NIV).

I can go on forever listing verse after verse because Proverbs is rich with great practical advice, but I wanted to know if my polling routine was a wise practice in its own right. This is where I moved past the directness of Proverbs and into other stories in Scripture to see if anyone made decisions the way I did by involving many people and how that practice worked out for them.

Girl, I found what I was looking for, and I was reminded how the book God designed for us to learn about Him and from Him is rich in love and help!

Solomon's son Rehoboam is a terrific study when evaluating the effects of too many suggestions, whom to ask and whom not to, and the consequences that invariably follow the advice you choose to take. After Solomon's death, Jeroboam, an administrator to the new king, appealed to Rehoboam on Israel's behalf: "Your father put a heavy yoke on us, but now lighten the harsh labor and the heavy yoke he put on us, and we will serve you" (1 Kings 12:4). The northern tribes were burdened with excessive taxation King Solomon had imposed in building his palace (1 Kings) along with other buildings (2 Chron. 8). Taxes were paid in various ways: money (silver or gold), a share of a person's crops, or labor toward construction:

> Rehoboam consulted the elders who had served his father, Solomon, during his lifetime. "How would you advise me to answer these people?" he asked. They replied, "If today you will be a servant to these people and serve them and give them a favorable answer, they will always be your servants." (1 Kings 12:6, 7 NIV)

I love that Solomon, a man God gave "a wise and discerning heart, so that there will never have been anyone like [him], nor will there ever be" (1 Kings 3:12), had elders he conferred with. Solomon understood the responsibilities and problems a leader faced would be a lonely road. The start of wisdom is to have other wise people around you, looking through the same perspective you are.

When seeking out advice or the approval of my choices, I talked to a diverse group of believers and nonbelievers. I went to people I knew were seeking God earnestly, people who didn't have a relationship with God, those who had never been affected by infertility, and those who had. Overall, I found less empathetic insight from people who had not dealt with infertility, and I had to defend what God was telling me from people who didn't consult God as a part of their decision-making process.

I tried to dig in to see if I could find any information on who the elders were that Rehoboam first brought his question to. Not much out there, but without creating a web of assumptions, I believe there are a few things we can infer:

1. The elders were established believers in Israel with a fear of the Lord.

2. They were older, with more experience and knowledge of historical decisions and their outcomes.

3. Solomon placed them to give himself council, making approaching them a safe place for Rehoboam to go.

Their advice is simply direct: serve to be served.

But Rehoboam rejected the advice the elders gave him and consulted the young men who had grown up with him and were serving him. He asked them, "What is your advice? How should we answer these people who say to me, 'Lighten the yoke your father put on us'?" The young men who had grown up with him replied, "These people have said to you, 'Your father put a heavy yoke on us, but make our yoke lighter.' Now tell them, 'My little finger is thicker than my father's waist. My father laid on you a heavy yoke; I will make it even heavier. My father scourged you with whips; I will scourge you with scorpions.'" (1 Kings 12:8–11 NIV)

First, I want to point out that when Rehoboam asked the elders, he said, "How do you advise *me* to answer?" (vs. 6), but when he invited his friends, he said, "What do you advise that *we* answer?" (8). Regardless of Rehoboam's choice, the decision will eventually be his to make, and he will be the only one to bear the weight of his answer fully. The same goes for the advice I collect and choose to follow. We will have no excuse, no one to blame in the end how we respond to the choices before us. I can't afford to consider everyone's opinions because it crowds out the voice of God. Instead of bogging myself down with popular belief, I need to go the shortest route to good advice. The relationships we establish are the community of people we build our lives around and often reflect ourselves.

Evaluating Rehoboam's second group he canvassed, we can see several red flags:

> 1. He grew up with them. They were all the same age and inexperienced.
>
> 2. They were described as "serving him." When I want to hear what I want to listen to, I know exactly who to go to, but that doesn't mean they'll speak the truth to me.
>
> 3. According to my ESV Bible, the phrase "My little finger is thicker than my father's thighs" is literally, in Hebrew, "My little one is thicker than my father's thighs," most likely a reference to his sexual organ rather than a literal finger (1). That makes these guys' responses incredibly childish and, therefore, dangerous.

Rehoboam only had himself in mind when searching out the answer that appealed to him. He foolishly chose to go with his friends' advice, eventually leading to the division of Israel as a united kingdom. Ten tribes went with Jeroboam, creating Israel, and the other two tribes left over (Judah and Benjamin) became the kingdom of Judea under Rehoboam's rule.

A part of accepting advice is knowing whom you're receiving it from; the other part is anticipating how the outcome will play out. I learned that it doesn't matter how many people's opinions I have because knowing them only brings me more confusion. Whom I choose to listen to needs to meet specific requirements:

1. God-fearing

2. Experienced

3. A record of wise counsel

- Whom do you depend on to give you advice?

- Can you determine what is advice and what is opinion?

- How does this story influence how you speak into other people's lives?

Untitled Intentionally

I'm sitting in the same place I was when I started writing this book, my oversize, saggy, brown chair-and-a-half in my living room. Currently, I don't have any answers or solutions. What I do have is the windows open, a fresh cup of coffee, and my yoga teacher's Spotify playlist pumping through my TV speakers. My eyes are open, and I'm looking around at my eclectically warm apartment with its browns, golds, baskets, and pictures, intermixed with POP cartoon figurine characters that Mike loves. The wind is blowing in, and my forever faithful dog, Wrigley, is at my feet. My diffuser is cranking out doTERRA's Balance blend with spruce leaf, blue tansy flower (my favorite), and blue chamomile flower. Writing while being present is my self-care today.

Last week wasn't an easy week. Caden started walking, making me sad that he's growing up in the blink of an eye, and his milestone made me wonder if I will ever have the opportunity to be a mom at the end of that first step. We are walking through homes, which overwhelmed me because I don't understand the process, or how to get organized and feel prepared. Part of me wants to take the easy route and remain in this comfortably small apartment, but that means I will be a willing participant in delaying our dreams. I cried a lot. I slept little. Each conversation we attempted seemed to break down into misunderstandings and disagreements. In this space now, I can see we were both fueled by grief and fear.

Satan taunted me with insecurities: Your sadness hurts Mike. You shouldn't tell him how you feel. Why do you allow yourself to cry so freely? Mike will get sick of it, and you'll grow apart. You don't make enough money. You should have earned a college degree. You won't be able to do this. You aren't prepared enough...

Guilt rode in, and I felt sad and angry that I couldn't change my perspective. Pummeling me even further were thoughts on how I should be more focused on how wonderful my marriage is; I should trust in God more; I should appreciate my home more because it is my sanctuary.

I'm slowly learning that *should* is a judgment, a word that perpetuates guilt and shame, turning beautiful, meaningful things into obligations and duties. Satan uses it as a way to criticize my actions. *Should* is placing myself against myself in defense of my feelings. I plan to change *should* to *choose*. I choose to focus on how wonderful my marriage is, and on those hard days, we did things we enjoyed doing together: we walked our pup, baked cookies, and watched stand-up comedy. I choose to trust God more, so I am praying about each house we see. If it's for us, I pray that God keeps it on the market until our lease is up, and if it doesn't stay on the market, to know and accept that answer. I choose to sit in my home, look around at my blessings, and realize that I'm not responsible for what God hasn't given me, but I am responsible for the people and things He has placed in my life. I want to leave the worry of failing behind us and pay attention to what the Lord is teaching us.

Today is about filling my cup. Tomorrow I might be screaming my battle cry, but girl, I promise you, the war paint is on! One of the reasons I began writing is because I haven't read a book yet that didn't have the end game. I haven't read a book written when someone was deep in this infertility struggle. (Not saying those don't exist, but who can read every book?) I am still in this with you. I'm learning to trust, to grieve, to be content. I'm letting God rename my chapter.

Mike and I are creating this life together; I chose him, and he chose me! This journey isn't over, but if he and I are hand in hand, waiting, watching, and trusting in God, we will continue to grow in wisdom and love, on the bad days and the good ones. And we aren't alone either, with terrific support from family and friends; whatever God has in store for us, we surely will rise to the occasion.

I'm praying for you. I may not know you by name, but we're connected in this infertility struggle. Please always remember to give yourself grace, honor what your needs are, create your support team, strengthen your marriage, and most importantly, fix your eyes on Jesus.

Blessings, my lovelies.

Works Cited

Chapman, Gary D. *The Five Love Languages: How to Express Heartfelt Commitment to Your Mate*. Nashville, TN, Lifeway Press, 2010.

"Dictionary.com | Meanings & Definitions of English Words." *Dictionary.com*, www.dictionary.com/browse/advice.

Extend Fertility. "IUI vs. IVF: The Procedures, Success Rates, and Costs." *Extend Fertility*, 3 Sept. 2020, extendfertility.com/iui-vs-ivf/.

Niequist, Shauna. *Present over Perfect*. Center Point Pub, 2017.

Psycom. "The Five Stages of Grief." *Psycom.net*, Psycom, 7 June 2022, www.psycom.net/stages-of-grief.

"The Definition of Journey." *www.dictionary.com*, 2019, www.dictionary.com/browse/journey.

NIV Bible. Grand Rapids, Mi, Zondervan Pub. House, 2011.

"Translating Assertive Language in 1 Kings 12:10–11." *Ancient Hebrew Poetry*, 2017, ancienthebrewpoetry.typepad.com/ancient_hebrew_poetry/2009/03/translating-assertive-language-in-1-kings-121011-.html#:~:text=The%20foolish%20advice%20of%20the.

NIV Verses listed in order :

- Proverbs 30:15, 16
- Ecclesiastes 7:13, 14
- Psalm 88 (rewritten)
- Romans 8:28
- Genesis 1:28
- John 15:5
- Exodus 16
- Exodus 13:21
- Exodus 14
- Exodus 15:22–25
- John 9:1–3
- 2 Samuel 12
- Ephesians 4:13
- Numbers 2:1–12
- Deuteronomy 34:1–6
- Matthew 22:12–13
- Matthew 14:22–32
- Acts 15:7–11
- Luke 18:10–14
- Matthew 7:26, 27
- Titus 3:5
- Acts 4:12
- Romans 3:27, 28
- 2 Corinthians 1:9
- John 6:28, 29
- James 2:10, 11
- Genesis 3:1–7
- Acts 2:42–47
- John 16:33
- Proverbs 17:22
- 2 Corinthians 1:3, 4
- Romans 11:6
- Hebrews 4:16
- John 1:16
- 1 Kings 16:29–34
- Matthew 19:5
- Ephesians 5:25
- Proverbs 27:17
- Luke 22:28
- Esther
- Proverbs 3:13
- Proverbs 8:11
- Proverbs 27:9
- John 15:13
- Proverbs 3:13–15
- Proverbs 4:5–9

- Proverbs 11:16
- Proverbs 11:25
- Proverbs 12:13
- Proverbs 15:1
- 1 Kings 12

www.ingramcontent.com/pod-product-compliance
Lightning Source LLC
LaVergne TN
LVHW092051060526
838201LV00047B/1339